First published in the United States of America in 2012 by

New York | London

322 West 57 Street, #19T
New York, NY 10019
Telephone: 212 362 9119

London Office:
1 Rona Road
London NW3 2HY
Tel/Fax +44 (0) 207 8339

www.GlitteratiIncorporated.com
media@GlitteratiIncorporated.com for inquiries

First edition, 2012
Library of Congress Cataloging-in-Publication
data is available from the publisher

Hardcover ISBN13: 978-0-9832702-4-9

Design and layout by the author
with Sarah Morgan Karp/smk-design.com
Edited by Judith Durant

Printed and bound in China
10 9 8 7 6 5 4 3 2 1

Knitologie

CREATING PERSONAL HEIRLOOM KNITS
AS SIMPLY AS CASTING ON AND CASTING OFF

Lucy Main Tweet

Glitterati
INCORPORATED

New York | London

Acknowledgments

To my Mom, Ann Main, whose creativity, sense of style and confidence
in me makes me realize that every day is a privilege and an opportunity.

To my husband, John Tweet, whose support and love mean everything to me.

To my brother, Robert Main, for his interest, confidence and guidance.

To my friend and former colleague Leslie Kingeter, for her help, support and
willingness to assist in every way possible.

To my friend and former colleague Krissy Blakeway, who gave me the idea
and stirred the passion to go forward with writing the book.

To my friend and former colleague Deborah Dines, the best knitter I know,
who gave me confidence and who tested several patterns for me.

To my friend Helen Spencer Ryan, whose zeal for life and can-do
attitude buoyed me along my literary ride.

To my friend Ione Louzada, whose confidence, challenges and
support kept me going.

To Kathy Fleischer, whose talent at a sewing machine made my
dreams come true and my projects come to life.

To Nina Karnes, who taught me the I.S. skills to assemble my manuscript.

To James Booth, whose help and support has meant so much.

To Marta and John, thank you for making this literary adventure so rewarding.

FOR MY MOM

Table of Concepts

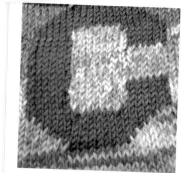

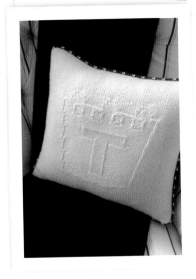

Introduction

My Story

I spent three decades of my time, energy and creative abilities in the fashion industry. It was a wonderful career, and I enjoyed it immensely. Initially my job had a creative bent, and then during the middle and later years I worked on the supply-chain side of the business. Both positions were incredibly challenging and rewarding, and I am proud to say that I have wonderful friends and former colleagues around the world who will be with me always.

When that chapter of my life ended in 2008, I found for the first time in my adult life the time and energy to pursue things that I'd never had the time to undertake. Throughout my professional career my personal passion was needlepoint. You might ask, "Where did you ever find the time?" The answer is simple: You would be amazed at the number of hours spent waiting in airport lounges and up at night with the dreaded jet lag. These time periods provided me with a great deal of opportunity to craft needlepoint projects. I amassed quite the collection of pillows, framed pictures and Christmas ornaments, and was able to share many of them with friends and family as gifts.

With so many changes in my life occurring at once, I decided to leave needlepoint and try something different. This is where my mom enters the picture — she suggested I try my hand at knitting. I must be honest and say that I'd tried knitting at other stages of my life but never stuck with it.

You might wonder why and the answer is, in part, the inspiration for this book. I was, and still am, a very novice knitter. I know four simple things:

1. How to cast on, in a non-conventional way

2. How to cast off

3. How to knit

4. How to purl.

So what can you make with these skills? I soon began to make everyone's favorite, scarves. Before long boredom set in, but everyone told me to get some cheap yarn and practice, practice, practice to become proficient enough to do something more complicated and interesting. My plain yarn in a basic color did not hold my interest, so I decided to follow my contrarian spirit.

A trip to a local yarn store yielded a very interesting yarn with texture and a gorgeous variegated color. This held more interest. Even if the knitting was not a success, I had made a relatively small investment in something captivating. However, after making several scarves, which actually did get used, the creative challenge was still missing. I decided to buy a pattern and try something different. This is where the real trouble began, which provided a reason for this book.

The abbreviations and the language of knitting patterns was mind-boggling and I would get lost in the pattern from one knitting session to the next. If a few days went by, I was hopelessly lost. Frustration nearly caused me to give up. That's when my creative DNA came through. It was essential to come up with a unique idea that would hold my interest.

Thoughts of my Grandmother Main were with me in the process. She appreciated high quality and was incredibly creative. She had created my first play dresses (yes, little girls wore dresses for play in the 1950s), stitched by hand from my grandfather's dress shirts. The button front of his shirt became the button back of my dress. The back yoke of his shirt was hand smocked to become the front of my dress. I love this story and believe the origins of this book are connected to that creativity. Talk about "personal" and "custom."

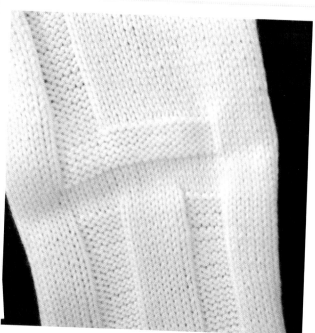

My mom also helped me in this process. She is another incredibly creative woman and you can read her thoughts about knitting later in this book. Now in her eighties, my mom knits several hours every day. She makes hats, and hats alone. That might sound boring to some of you, but if you could see the hats you'd see that each and every one is different, and you'd understand how her creative passion is served.

With these two wonderful women as inspiration, I decided that personalization would be my path. Actually, it has always been a part of my life, from mono-grammed clothing to personalized stationary to engraved flatware. My initials, LAM in the beginning and later LMT, have always been a big part of my life. Many of my formerprofessional colleagues did not call me Lucy, or Mrs. Tweet. They called me L-M-T.

And so, I thought, I can make a scarf. Yes, I said scarf, but one that uses my initials! So with a piece of ordinary graph paper and pencil, L, M and T were born. The background would be knit and the letters would be purl. Very subtle and easy, and theses letters would not require a contrast color or intarsia proficiency. Remember, I am a novice knitter with limited skills. I found a beautiful yarn in a great color and began knitting.

It soon became obvious that L, M and T did not make a very big scarf, so I decided to repeat it once, repeat it twice and continue until I reached the desired length. It worked! There was nothing like it in any pattern book, and my scarf was mine and mine alone. It was easy, rewarding and different.

Several weeks later, L, M and T having been mastered, I thought, "What about a scarf that has my entire name — Lucy Main Tweet?" I crafted the required letters on my trusty graph paper and set about making a new scarf. This worked well and I was still challenged, still rewarded, and in the end I had something that was uniquely my own.

This is where things got interesting. With two scarves for me and one for my husband, J-A-T, I looked around my house for inspiration and found my old needlepoint projects. This led to the idea of personalizing pillows to decorate the house. Remember, I only know four things about knitting, so I wanted to expand on the idea that had already provided excitement. I started relatively small, with a T on a small pillow similar in size to ones that I had done in needlepoint. Well, that was fun, now what? So I started doing multiple letters, i.e., L, M and T in multiple rows. This led to a four-quadrant pillow with my full initials. While doing all of this, I played around with different backgrounds utilizing only my trusty knit and purl. I used colors that would coordinate with our house, since my husband is an interior decorator and would not have it any other way! With each idea came another, and then another.

While on the phone with my mom, the baby hat specialist, we came up with the idea to focus on babies and create wonderful future heirlooms and gifts. Since I'd begun my career in children's apparel, it seemed right to have a collection of baby patterns. Caps are the focus, in honor of my mom, but there are other styles that allow for single letter usage, or combinations.

This book also includes some of my must haves, favorite things and tips that came to mind while working the patterns. Several projects have been done in multiples and, honestly, many are fast and easy. In just a few hours you can have a family heirloom. Each pattern includes a space for you to keep track of the project and/or the letter multiple times.

This book has been a wonderful adventure for me and I truly hope that you enjoy both the photography and the knitting patterns. The layout and presentation is intended to encourage creativity and nurture family. All of this was possible because of a skill my mother shared with me. Thanks Mom, for your patience. I'm sure you didn't expect that I would ever write a knitting book, especially when thinking of those days, decades ago, when I'd come to you with the latest round of problems and mistakes!

My mother has been a wonderful help to me throughout this process and without her involvement it never would have happened. Our relationship has grown and grown, and there are not enough pages in this book to share with you the laughs we've had. Because of this, I hope that there will be many of you who will share this creative pastime with your children or your grandchildren.

In one of the final editions of *Southern Accents* magazine, monograms were featured in the Gracious Living and Entertainment section. I loved what they said:

> *Monograms. . .a mark of identification has turned into a symbol of living well and a vehicle for expressing creativity on everything from bed linens to tote bags. Personal and timeless, the monogram can elevate everyday objects to one-of-a -kind items.*

I hope you remember these words and that you find hours of pleasure as you page through the book and determine the project that is best for you. The patterns are just the beginning and it is up to you to make each project yours and yours alone. Be proud of your name, initials and monogram. They are a part of what makes you an individual and your projects personal and timeless.

All the best and enjoy,

A JOURNEY IN STITCHES: SPECIAL THOUGHTS FROM MY MOM

> An older French-speaking lady showed me how to knit using two extra-long construction nails and a length of household twine.

> A favorite aunt bought me my first real needles and real yarn downstairs in J.J. Newberry's.

> My sixth grade teacher, Mrs. Fayette, whom I loved, crocheted each of her pupils a small pouch upon graduation. That prompted me to knit small pouches with a crocheted drawstring for jewelry bags.

> My first finished effort was socks on four needles.

> My boyfriend, who later became my husband, wore eleven pair of argyle socks and single design (one-color cable or other texture) socks that I knitted for him over the years.

> Many stitches later, baby booties, caps and mittens came on the scene followed by ski caps, mittens and scarfs for my family and friends.

> Over the years, my repertoire expanded to miniature sweaters for my daughter's Barbie doll collection and caps for the maternity ward of the Alice Hyde Memorial Center.

> The last few stitches are found in baby caps and pacifier pouches for the babies of friends of my children and have given me the tolerance for the limitations of old age.

Coco

Cast On Cast Off is the name I came up with for my knitting endeavors. When initialized, those words spell COCO, and Coco is the name of my very special friend pictured above. Coco is an nine-year-old Coton du Tulear, which is a cousin of the Bichon Frise and the Maltese.

Since entering our lives, Coco has brought nothing but joy, comfort, happiness and laughter. She has been a part of this project since the beginning, sitting at my feet or next to me on the couch as I knit. She has wanted to be a part of nearly every photo and she has inspected all of my yarns.

In addition to letter grids, I've included a paw print graph that will allow you to craft a project in honor of your favorite four-legged friend!

Coco Tweet was born on
October 12, 2003. This book
would not be complete
without a signature design in
her honor. You too can knit
a signature for your special
friend with this grid.

*A larger paw print grid is
available on page 63.*

Row 10		
Row 9		
Row 8		
Row 7		
Row 6		
Row 5		
Row 4		
Row 3		
Row 2		
Row 1	✓	

			*			*		
			*			*		
	*		*			*		*
	*							*
	*		*	*	*	*		*
		*	*	*	*	*	*	
	*	*	*	*	*	*	*	*
	*	*	*	*	*	*	*	*
		*	*	*	*	*	*	
			*	*	*	*		

Needles

I work with Clover brand
Takumi Bamboo Premium
and Brittany needles.

$\mathcal{Y}$arns

It's a good idea to keep a record of your favorite yarns; I keep all of my yarn labels in one glass canister. You'll be amazed at how often you go back to reference a particular yarn months after the initial purchase. It's also convenient if you have underestimated the required yarn amount on a specific project and need to find more of the exact color and dye lot number. Color availability, method of washing, feel to the touch and cost will all factor into which yarns become your personal favorites — here are some of mine.

> Berroco Ultra Alpaca
  50 % alpaca/50 % wool
  5 stitches per inch on
  US 8 (5 mm) needles

> blue sky alpacas Worsted Cotton
  100 % organic cotton
  4–5 stitches per inch on
  US 7–9 (4.5–5.5 mm) needles

> Classic Elite Yarns Charmed
  85 % cashmere/15% mohair
  4.5 stitches per inch on
  US 8 (5 mm) needles

> Debbie Bliss cashmerino aran
  55 % merino wool/
  33 % microfiber/12 % cashmere
  4.5 stitches per inch
  on US 8 (5 mm) needles

> Frog Tree Pima Silk Sport Weight
  85% pima cotton/15 % silk
  5 stitches per inch on
  US 5 (3.75 mm) needles

> Grace Wool and Silk by Louisa Harding
  50% merino wool/50% silk
  5.5 stitches per inch on
  US 6 (4 mm) needles

> jil eaton minnow merino —
  Classic Elite Yarns
  100% extra fine merino wool
  4.5 stitches pre inch on
  US 8 (5 mm) needles

> Lorna's Laces Shepherd Bulky
  100 % superwash wool
  3.5 stitches per inch on
  US 10 (6 mm) needles

> Lorna's Laces Shepherd Worsted
  100% superwash wool
  4.5 stitches per inch on
  US 7 (4.5 mm) needles

> Mary Jo Cole (private brand)
  100% cashmere
  4.5 stitches per inch on
  US 8 (5 mm) needles

> Tahki Cotton Classic —
  Tahki Stacy Charles, Inc.
  100% mercerized cotton
  4.75–5 stitches per inch on
  US 6–7 (4–4.5 mm) needles

Tools
Must-Have Knitting Tools You Will Use Again and Again

1   Yarns should always be carefully selected.
     They're going to be your friends for awhile!

2   Stitch holders are essential in order to make
     the mittens in this book.

3   Rubber tips for your needles are lifesavers; they
     prevent your stitches from falling off the needles.

4   Markers keep track of your rows, which is key,
     especially when you're knitting on a circular needle.

5   Darning needles (with a large eye) will make
     securing loose ends very easy.

6   Needle selection is very important; you must
     be comfortable with them.

7   Paper kept close at hand is a wonderful aid;
     use it to jot down your status and ideas.

8   Pencils are just the best as they allow you
     to fix, embellish or change your mind.

9   Scissors should always be close at hand;
     round nose models can still go on planes.

10   Measuring tapes help to track your status.

Color Concepts

When it comes to making choices for your first, second or later projects, it's best to look to your own surroundings for inspiration. For this book I looked to my closet and around my home.

BLUE & WHITE

I love these colors in clothes. Navy and white are my favorite staples, regardless of the season. My home, indoors and out, is filled with blue and white porcelain. From ginger jars to planters to plates and saucers, they all recall wonderful memories of past trips to Asia and the people and places that are a part of those wonderful memories. I always have my eye out for magazines or books with blue and white inspirations for me and for our home. Many of my lifestyle icons such as Carolyne Roehm, Charlotte Moss, Ina Garten and Bunny Williams have done features on blue and white.

YELLOW & BLUE

This love affair is a direct extension of my interest in blue and white. I discovered this wonderful combination in multiple shapes and sizes while visiting a porcelain shop in Hong Kong many years ago. These colors dominated the living room in one of our homes and I have done many needlepoint projects focusing on them. Now I enjoy knitting them alone or in combination.

GRAY, GRAY & MORE GRAY

When I used to travel extensively for business, one of the tricks I learned was to pick a color of clothing for my trip. It made mixing and matching so much easier and it certainly cut down on the number of shoes that I needed to bring with me. Several members of my old team used to kid me and ask, "Is this a gray trip or a navy trip?" Today my travels are more personally focused but this trick has become my standard way to pack.

Gray is very versatile and comes in many shades, both solid and tweed. My attraction to this color has origins in my home where silver accessories are everywhere. Sterling candlesticks, hollowware and other accessories should come out of the storage chests and closets to be enjoyed. I've recently developed an interest in mercury glass, another silver cast medium. My first purchase was a piece for Christmas decorating, but it looked so great with my blue and white Christmas ornaments that I thought, "Why use it only for a few weeks a year?" That piece, and more, found their way into my home for good.

CREAM, CAMEL & KHAKI

This is another favorite color story from my wardrobe and my home and it offers many possibilities. What is more classic, more tasteful, than a simple pair of khaki pants and a crisp white shirt! Add a pashmina in an accent color and you can go anywhere, anytime.

This colorway is also reminiscent of wonderful basketry from around the world. Whether it is wood from Vermont, sea grass from Charleston or ate (pronounced ah-tay) from Bali, each has color tones that fit into this universal palette.

As you can see, my posses-
sions are my inspiration. I
hope yours inspire you. You
are one of a kind. Embrace
and enjoy it. The possibilities
are endless!

SPECIAL OCCASION COLORS

Pink for girls, blue for boys, red and green for Christmas, blue and
white for Hanukkah, orange and black for Halloween and red, white
and blue for all patriotic holidays — having these colors stored in
canisters by category is a great way to be prepared for a special event.

Letter Grids

The following pages of the book comprise knitting stitch grids for every letter of the alphabet, and a paw print! These are the tools that will allow you to customize whichever knitting pattern you choose.

Each large grid uses the actual letter as a symbol, as opposed to using symbols for knit or purl stitches. This format allows you to determine how you want your alphabet to be knit. For example, you have the choice to have a purl background with a knit letter or a knit background with a purl letter. This also enables you to use the alternatives in combination, especially if you are knitting the cube or other patchwork type patterns. You also have flexibility to change stitches depending on the trim or border stitch that you're using. This is entirely a matter of choice and your opportunity to make each and every project yours and yours alone.

Because they'll be knitted, all letters and numbers are basic in design to allow for maximum detail. Some of the designs may appear a bit elongated but when actually knit, I'm confident you will be pleased with the result.

Medium letter grids are also provided for use on several patterns with the baby projects. Their layout is smaller in order to best accommodate the smaller projects. These grids are half the size of their larger counterparts: 10 stitches across and 14 rows up and down. Use the grids alone or in tandem with the larger letters to create a monogram — it's entirely up to you!

Every grid is specific to the letter and does not include any background. The project patterns are presented row by row, with a portion designated as "customize 20," meaning that you knit your chosen letter from the grid over these 20 stitches. Other patterns provide a generic letter or letters, but once again you can easily customize them to suit your needs.

Knitting chart — Row 1 (bottom) to Row 28 (top).

Left tracking grid:

Row 28				
Row 27				
Row 26				
Row 25				
Row 24				
Row 23				
Row 22				
Row 21				
Row 20				
Row 19				
Row 18				
Row 17				
Row 16				
Row 15				
Row 14				
Row 13				
Row 12				
Row 11				
Row 10				
Row 9				
Row 8				
Row 7				
Row 6				
Row 5				
Row 4				
Row 3		✓		
Row 2				
Row 1				

Chart grid (19 columns):

Row	1	2	3	4	5	6	7	8	9	10	11	12	13	14	15	16	17	18	19
Row 28									a	a	a	a							
Row 27									a	a	a	a							
Row 26									a	a	a	a							
Row 25									a	a	a	a							
Row 24								a	a	a	a	a	a						
Row 23								a	a	a	a	a	a						
Row 22								a	a	a	a	a	a						
Row 21							a	a	a	a	a	a	a	a					
Row 20							a	a	a	a	a	a	a	a					
Row 19							a	a	a	a	a	a	a						
Row 18						a	a	a	a					a	a	a	a		
Row 17						a	a	a	a					a	a	a	a		
Row 16						a	a	a						a	a	a			
Row 15					a	a	a	a						a	a	a	a		
Row 14					a	a	a							a	a	a			
Row 13					a	a	a	a	a	a	a	a	a	a	a	a			
Row 12				a	a	a	a	a	a	a	a	a	a	a	a	a	a		
Row 11				a	a	a	a	a	a	a	a	a	a	a	a	a	a		
Row 10				a	a	a	a	a	a	a	a	a	a	a	a	a	a		
Row 9		a	a	a	a	a	a	a	a	a	a	a	a	a	a	a	a		
Row 8		a	a	a	a	a	a						a	a	a	a	a	a	
Row 7		a	a	a	a	a	a						a	a	a	a	a	a	
Row 6		a	a	a	a	a	a							a	a	a	a	a	a
Row 5		a	a	a	a	a	a							a	a	a	a	a	a
Row 4		a	a	a	a	a									a	a	a	a	a
Row 3	a	a	a	a	a	a								a	a	a	a	a	a
Row 2	a	a	a	a											a	a	a	a	a
Row 1	a	a	a	a	a										a	a	a	a	a

Row 28				
Row 27				
Row 26				
Row 25				
Row 24				
Row 23				
Row 22				
Row 21				
Row 20				
Row 19				
Row 18				
Row 17				
Row 16				
Row 15				
Row 14				
Row 13				
Row 12				
Row 11				
Row 10				
Row 9				
Row 8				
Row 7				
Row 6				
Row 5				
Row 4				
Row 3				
Row 2		✓		
Row 1	✓			

Row 28: b b b b b b b b b b b b b b b b
Row 27: b b b b b b b b b b b b b b b b b
Row 26: b b b b b b b b b b b b b b b b b b
Row 25: b b b b b b b b b b b b b b b b b b b
Row 24: b b b b b b b b b b b b b b b b b b b b
Row 23: b b b b b b   b b b b b b b b
Row 22: b b b b b b   b b b b b b b
Row 21: b b b b b b   b b b b b b
Row 20: b b b b b b   b b b b b b
Row 19: b b b b b b   b b b b b b
Row 18: b b b b b b   b b b b b b b
Row 17: b b b b b b   b b b b b b b
Row 16: b b b b b b b b b b b b b b b b b b
Row 15: b b b b b b b b b b b b b b b b b
Row 14: b b b b b b b b b b b b b b b b b
Row 13: b b b b b b b b b b b b b b b b b b b
Row 12: b b b b b b b b b b b b b b b b b b b b
Row 11: b b b b b b   b b b b b b b b
Row 10: b b b b b b   b b b b b b b
Row 9: b b b b b b   b b b b b b b
Row 8: b b b b b b   b b b b b b b
Row 7: b b b b b b   b b b b b b b
Row 6: b b b b b b   b b b b b b b
Row 5: b b b b b b   b b b b b b b b
Row 4: b b b b b b b b b b b b b b b b b b
Row 3: b b b b b b b b b b b b b b b b b b b
Row 2: b b b b b b b b b b b b b b b b b b
Row 1: b b b b b b b b b b b b b b b b b

	1	2	3	4	5	6	7	8	9	10	11	12	13	14	15	16	17	18	19	20	21
Row 28			c	c	c	c	c	c	c	c	c	c	c	c	c	c	c	c	c		
Row 27		c	c	c	c	c	c	c	c	c	c	c	c	c	c	c	c	c	c	c	
Row 26	c	c	c	c	c	c	c	c	c	c	c	c	c	c	c	c	c	c	c	c	c
Row 25	c	c	c	c	c	c	c	c	c	c	c	c	c	c	c	c	c	c	c	c	c
Row 24	c	c	c	c	c	c	c	c	c	c	c	c	c	c	c	c	c	c	c	c	c
Row 23	c	c	c	c	c	c	c	c	c	c	c	c	c	c	c	c	c	c	c	c	c
Row 22	c	c	c	c	c	c	c	c								c	c	c	c	c	c
Row 21	c	c	c	c	c	c										c	c	c	c	c	c
Row 20	c	c	c	c	c	c										c	c	c	c	c	c
Row 19	c	c	c	c	c	c										c	c	c	c	c	c
Row 18	c	c	c	c	c	c										c	c	c	c	c	c
Row 17	c	c	c	c	c	c															
Row 16	c	c	c	c	c	c															
Row 15	c	c	c	c	c	c															
Row 14	c	c	c	c	c	c															
Row 13	c	c	c	c	c	c															
Row 12	c	c	c	c	c	c															
Row 11	c	c	c	c	c	c										c	c	c	c	c	c
Row 10	c	c	c	c	c	c										c	c	c	c	c	c
Row 9	c	c	c	c	c	c										c	c	c	c	c	c
Row 8	c	c	c	c	c	c										c	c	c	c	c	c
Row 7	c	c	c	c	c	c	c								c	c	c	c	c	c	c
Row 6	c	c	c	c	c	c	c	c	c	c	c	c	c	c	c	c	c	c	c	c	c
Row 5	c	c	c	c	c	c	c	c	c	c	c	c	c	c	c	c	c	c	c	c	c
Row 4	c	c	c	c	c	c	c	c	c	c	c	c	c	c	c	c	c	c	c	c	c
Row 3	c	c	c	c	c	c	c	c	c	c	c	c	c	c	c	c	c	c	c	c	c
Row 2		c	c	c	c	c	c	c	c	c	c	c	c	c	c	c	c	c	c	c	
Row 1			c	c	c	c	c	c	c	c	c	c	c	c	c	c	c	c	c		

(Left tracking grid: Row 1 marked with a checkmark ✓)

Row 28				
Row 27				
Row 26				
Row 25				
Row 24				
Row 23				
Row 22				
Row 21				
Row 20				
Row 19				
Row 18				
Row 17				
Row 16				
Row 15				
Row 14				
Row 13				
Row 12				
Row 11				
Row 10				
Row 9				
Row 8				
Row 7				
Row 6				
Row 5				
Row 4				
Row 3				
Row 2				
Row 1	✓			

Row 28: d d d d d d d d d d d d d d d d
Row 27: d d d d d d d d d d d d d d d d d
Row 26: d d d d d d d d d d d d d d d d d d
Row 25: d d d d d d d d d d d d d d d d d d
Row 24: d d d d d d d d d d d d d d d d d d
Row 23: d d d d d d d d d d d d d d d d d d
Row 22: d d d d d d   d d d d d d d
Row 21: d d d d d d   d d d d d d
Row 20: d d d d d d   d d d d d d
Row 19: d d d d d d   d d d d d d
Row 18: d d d d d d   d d d d d d
Row 17: d d d d d d   d d d d d d
Row 16: d d d d d d   d d d d d d
Row 15: d d d d d d   d d d d d d
Row 14: d d d d d d   d d d d d d
Row 13: d d d d d d   d d d d d d
Row 12: d d d d d d   d d d d d d
Row 11: d d d d d d   d d d d d d
Row 10: d d d d d d   d d d d d d
Row 9: d d d d d d   d d d d d d
Row 8: d d d d d d   d d d d d d
Row 7: d d d d d d   d d d d d d d
Row 6: d d d d d d d d d d d d d d d d
Row 5: d d d d d d d d d d d d d d d d
Row 4: d d d d d d d d d d d d d d d d d
Row 3: d d d d d d d d d d d d d d d d d
Row 2: d d d d d d d d d d d d d d d d d
Row 1: d d d d d d d d d d d d d d d d

Row 28				
Row 27				
Row 26				
Row 25				
Row 24				
Row 23				
Row 22				
Row 21				
Row 20				
Row 19				
Row 18				
Row 17				
Row 16				
Row 15				
Row 14				
Row 13				
Row 12				
Row 11				
Row 10				
Row 9				
Row 8				
Row 7				
Row 6				
Row 5				
Row 4				
Row 3				
Row 2				
Row 1	✓			

Chart (Row 28 at top, Row 1 at bottom):

```
Row 28: e e e e e e e e e e e e e e e e e e e e
Row 27: e e e e e e e e e e e e e e e e e e e e
Row 26: e e e e e e e e e e e e e e e e e e e e
Row 25: e e e e e e e e e e e e e e e e e e e e
Row 24: e e e e e e e e e e e e e e e e e e e e
Row 23: e e e e e e e e e e e e e e e e e e e e
Row 22: e e e e e
Row 21: e e e e e
Row 20: e e e e e
Row 19: e e e e e
Row 18: e e e e e
Row 17: e e e e e
Row 16: e e e e e e e e e e
Row 15: e e e e e e e e e e e
Row 14: e e e e e e e e e e
Row 13: e e e e e e e e e e e
Row 12: e e e e e
Row 11: e e e e e
Row 10: e e e e e
Row 9:  e e e e e
Row 8:  e e e e e
Row 7:  e e e e e
Row 6:  e e e e e e e e e e e e e e e e e e e e
Row 5:  e e e e e e e e e e e e e e e e e e e e
Row 4:  e e e e e e e e e e e e e e e e e e e e
Row 3:  e e e e e e e e e e e e e e e e e e e e
Row 2:  e e e e e e e e e e e e e e e e e e e e
Row 1:  e e e e e e e e e e e e e e e e e e e e
```

Row 28				
Row 27				
Row 26				
Row 25				
Row 24				
Row 23				
Row 22				
Row 21				
Row 20				
Row 19				
Row 18				
Row 17				
Row 16				
Row 15				
Row 14				
Row 13				
Row 12				
Row 11				
Row 10				
Row 9				
Row 8				
Row 7				
Row 6				
Row 5				
Row 4				
Row 3				
Row 2				
Row 1	✓			

Pattern chart (reading rows 28 down to 1):

- Row 28: f f f f f f f f f f f f f f f f f f f f
- Row 27: f f f f f f f f f f f f f f f f f f f f
- Row 26: f f f f f f f f f f f f f f f f f f f f
- Row 25: f f f f f f f f f f f f f f f f f f f f
- Row 24: f f f f f f f f f f f f f f f f f f f f
- Row 23: f f f f f f f f f f f f f f f f f f f f
- Row 22: f f f f f f
- Row 21: f f f f f f
- Row 20: f f f f f f
- Row 19: f f f f f f
- Row 18: f f f f f f
- Row 17: f f f f f f
- Row 16: f f f f f f f f f f f
- Row 15: f f f f f f f f f f f
- Row 14: f f f f f f f f f f f
- Row 13: f f f f f f f f f f f
- Row 12: f f f f f f
- Row 11: f f f f f f
- Row 10: f f f f f f
- Row 9: f f f f f f
- Row 8: f f f f f f
- Row 7: f f f f f f
- Row 6: f f f f f f
- Row 5: f f f f f f
- Row 4: f f f f f f
- Row 3: f f f f f f
- Row 2: f f f f f f
- Row 1: f f f f f f

Row 28				
Row 27				
Row 26				
Row 25				
Row 24				
Row 23				
Row 22				
Row 21				
Row 20				
Row 19				
Row 18				
Row 17				
Row 16				
Row 15				
Row 14				
Row 13				
Row 12				
Row 11				
Row 10				
Row 9				
Row 8				
Row 7				
Row 6				
Row 5				
Row 4				
Row 3				
Row 2				
Row 1	✓			

		g	g	g	g	g	g	g	g	g	g	g	g	g	g	g	g		
	g	g	g	g	g	g	g	g	g	g	g	g	g	g	g	g	g	g	
g	g	g	g	g	g	g	g	g	g	g	g	g	g	g	g	g	g	g	g
g	g	g	g	g	g	g	g	g	g	g	g	g	g	g	g	g	g	g	g
g	g	g	g	g	g	g	g	g	g	g	g	g	g	g	g	g	g	g	g
g	g	g	g	g	g	g	g	g	g	g	g	g	g	g	g	g	g	g	g
g	g	g	g	g	g	g							g	g	g	g	g	g	g
g	g	g	g	g	g									g	g	g	g	g	g
g	g	g	g	g	g									g	g	g	g	g	g
g	g	g	g	g	g									g	g	g	g	g	g
g	g	g	g	g	g									g	g	g	g	g	g
g	g	g	g	g	g														
g	g	g	g	g	g														
g	g	g	g	g	g				g	g	g	g	g	g	g	g	g	g	g
g	g	g	g	g	g				g	g	g	g	g	g	g	g	g	g	g
g	g	g	g	g	g				g	g	g	g	g	g	g	g	g	g	g
g	g	g	g	g	g							g	g	g	g	g			
g	g	g	g	g	g							g	g	g	g	g			
g	g	g	g	g	g								g	g	g	g	g		
g	g	g	g	g	g								g	g	g	g	g		
g	g	g	g	g	g									g	g	g	g	g	
g	g	g	g	g	g	g							g	g	g	g	g	g	
g	g	g	g	g	g	g	g	g	g	g	g	g	g	g	g	g	g	g	g
g	g	g	g	g	g	g	g	g	g	g	g	g	g	g	g	g	g	g	g
g	g	g	g	g	g	g	g	g	g	g	g	g	g	g	g	g	g	g	g
g	g	g	g	g	g	g	g	g	g	g	g	g	g	g	g	g	g	g	g
	g	g	g	g	g	g	g	g	g	g	g	g	g	g	g	g	g	g	
		g	g	g	g	g	g	g	g	g	g	g	g	g	g	g	g		

Row 28				
Row 27				
Row 26				
Row 25				
Row 24				
Row 23				
Row 22				
Row 21				
Row 20				
Row 19				
Row 18				
Row 17			.	
Row 16				
Row 15				
Row 14				
Row 13				
Row 12				
Row 11				
Row 10				
Row 9				
Row 8				
Row 7				
Row 6				
Row 5				
Row 4				
Row 3				
Row 2				
Row 1	✓			

Knitting chart (Row 28 at top → Row 1 at bottom):

Row 28	h h h h h h			h h h h h h
Row 27	h h h h h h			h h h h h h
Row 26	h h h h h h			h h h h h h
Row 25	h h h h h h			h h h h h h
Row 24	h h h h h h			h h h h h h
Row 23	h h h h h h			h h h h h h
Row 22	h h h h h h			h h h h h h
Row 21	h h h h h h			h h h h h h
Row 20	h h h h h h			h h h h h h
Row 19	h h h h h h			h h h h h h
Row 18	h h h h h h			h h h h h h
Row 17	h h h h h h			h h h h h h
Row 16	h h h h h h h h h h h h h h h h h h h h h h h h
Row 15	h h h h h h h h h h h h h h h h h h h h h h h h
Row 14	h h h h h h h h h h h h h h h h h h h h h h h h
Row 13	h h h h h h h h h h h h h h h h h h h h h h h h
Row 12	h h h h h h			h h h h h h
Row 11	h h h h h h			h h h h h h
Row 10	h h h h h h			h h h h h h
Row 9	h h h h h h			h h h h h h
Row 8	h h h h h h			h h h h h h
Row 7	h h h h h h			h h h h h h
Row 6	h h h h h h			h h h h h h
Row 5	h h h h h h			h h h h h h
Row 4	h h h h h h			h h h h h h
Row 3	h h h h h h			h h h h h h
Row 2	h h h h h h			h h h h h h
Row 1	h h h h h h			h h h h h h

Row 28				
Row 27				
Row 26				
Row 25				
Row 24				
Row 23				
Row 22				
Row 21				
Row 20				
Row 19				
Row 18				
Row 17				
Row 16				
Row 15				
Row 14				
Row 13				
Row 12				
Row 11				
Row 10				
Row 9				
Row 8				
Row 7				
Row 6				
Row 5				
Row 4				
Row 3				
Row 2				
Row 1	✓			

Right grid:

i	i	i	i	i	i	i	i	i	i	i	i	i	i	i	i	i	i	i	i
i	i	i	i	i	i	i	i	i	i	i	i	i	i	i	i	i	i	i	i
i	i	i	i	i	i	i	i	i	i	i	i	i	i	i	i	i	i	i	i
i	i	i	i	i	i	i	i	i	i	i	i	i	i	i	i	i	i	i	i
i	i	i	i	i	i	i	i	i	i	i	i	i	i	i	i	i	i	i	i
i	i	i	i	i	i	i	i	i	i	i	i	i	i	i	i	i	i	i	i
						i	i	i	i	i	i								
						i	i	i	i	i	i								
						i	i	i	i	i	i								
						i	i	i	i	i	i								
						i	i	i	i	i	i								
						i	i	i	i	i	i								
						i	i	i	i	i	i								
						i	i	i	i	i	i								
						i	i	i	i	i	i								
						i	i	i	i	i	i								
						i	i	i	i	i	i								
						i	i	i	i	i	i								
						i	i	i	i	i	i								
						i	i	i	i	i	i								
						i	i	i	i	i	i								
						i	i	i	i	i	i								
i	i	i	i	i	i	i	i	i	i	i	i	i	i	i	i	i	i	i	i
i	i	i	i	i	i	i	i	i	i	i	i	i	i	i	i	i	i	i	i
i	i	i	i	i	i	i	i	i	i	i	i	i	i	i	i	i	i	i	i
i	i	i	i	i	i	i	i	i	i	i	i	i	i	i	i	i	i	i	i
i	i	i	i	i	i	i	i	i	i	i	i	i	i	i	i	i	i	i	i
i	i	i	i	i	i	i	i	i	i	i	i	i	i	i	i	i	i	i	i

Row 28				
Row 27				
Row 26				
Row 25				
Row 24				
Row 23				
Row 22				
Row 21				
Row 20				
Row 19				
Row 18				
Row 17				
Row 16				
Row 15				
Row 14				
Row 13				
Row 12				
Row 11				
Row 10				
Row 9				
Row 8				
Row 7				
Row 6				
Row 5				
Row 4				
Row 3				
Row 2				
Row 1	✓			

Chart:

j	j	j	j	j	j	j	j	j	j	j	j	j	j	j	j	j	j	j
j	j	j	j	j	j	j	j	j	j	j	j	j	j	j	j	j	j	j
j	j	j	j	j	j	j	j	j	j	j	j	j	j	j	j	j	j	j
j	j	j	j	j	j	j	j	j	j	j	j	j	j	j	j	j	j	j
j	j	j	j	j	j	j	j	j	j	j	j	j	j	j	j	j	j	j
j	j	j	j	j	j	j	j	j	j	j	j	j	j	j	j	j	j	j
								j	j	j	j	j	j					
								j	j	j	j	j	j					
								j	j	j	j	j	j					
								j	j	j	j	j	j					
								j	j	j	j	j	j					
								j	j	j	j	j	j					
								j	j	j	j	j	j					
								j	j	j	j	j	j					
								j	j	j	j	j	j					
								j	j	j	j	j	j					
								j	j	j	j	j	j					
								j	j	j	j	j	j					
								j	j	j	j	j	j					
								j	j	j	j	j	j					
								j	j	j	j	j	j					
								j	j	j	j	j	j					
j	j	j	j	j				j	j	j	j	j	j					
j	j	j	j	j				j	j	j	j	j	j					
j	j	j	j	j				j	j	j	j	j	j					
j	j	j	j	j				j	j	j	j	j	j					
j	j	j	j	j	j	j		j	j	j	j	j	j					
	j	j	j	j	j	j	j	j	j	j	j							

Row 28				
Row 27				
Row 26				
Row 25				
Row 24				
Row 23				
Row 22				
Row 21				
Row 20				
Row 19				
Row 18				
Row 17				
Row 16				
Row 15				
Row 14				
Row 13				
Row 12				
Row 11				
Row 10				
Row 9				
Row 8				
Row 7				
Row 6				
Row 5				
Row 4				
Row 3				
Row 2	✓			
Row 1	✓			

1	2	3	4	5	6	7	8	9	10	11	12	13	14	15	16	17
k	k	k	k	k	k							k	k	k	k	k
k	k	k	k	k								k	k	k	k	k
k	k	k	k	k								k	k	k	k	
k	k	k	k	k								k	k	k	k	
k	k	k	k	k							k	k	k	k		
k	k	k	k	k							k	k	k	k		
k	k	k	k	k						k	k	k	k			
k	k	k	k	k	k					k	k	k	k			
k	k	k	k	k						k	k	k	k			
k	k	k	k	k					k	k	k	k	k			
k	k	k	k	k				k	k	k	k	k				
k	k	k	k	k			k	k	k	k	k					
k	k	k	k	k		k	k	k	k	k	k					
k	k	k	k	k	k	k	k	k	k	k						
k	k	k	k	k	k	k	k	k	k	k						
k	k	k	k	k	k		k	k	k	k	k					
k	k	k	k	k	k			k	k	k	k	k				
k	k	k	k	k	k				k	k	k	k	k			
k	k	k	k	k	k					k	k	k	k	k		
k	k	k	k	k	k						k	k	k	k		
k	k	k	k	k	k						k	k	k	k		
k	k	k	k	k	k						k	k	k	k		
k	k	k	k	k	k							k	k	k	k	
k	k	k	k	k	k							k	k	k	k	
k	k	k	k	k								k	k	k	k	
k	k	k	k	k								k	k	k	k	
k	k	k	k	k								k	k	k	k	k
k	k	k	k	k								k	k	k	k	k

Row 28				
Row 27				
Row 26				
Row 25				
Row 24				
Row 23				
Row 22				
Row 21				
Row 20				
Row 19				
Row 18				
Row 17				
Row 16				
Row 15				
Row 14				
Row 13				
Row 12				
Row 11				
Row 10				
Row 9				
Row 8				
Row 7				
Row 6				
Row 5				
Row 4				
Row 3				
Row 2	✓			
Row 1	✓			

Row 28: 1 1 1 1 1 1
Row 27: 1 1 1 1 1 1
Row 26: 1 1 1 1 1 1
Row 25: 1 1 1 1 1 1
Row 24: 1 1 1 1 1 1
Row 23: 1 1 1 1 1 1
Row 22: 1 1 1 1 1 1
Row 21: 1 1 1 1 1 1
Row 20: 1 1 1 1 1 1
Row 19: 1 1 1 1 1 1
Row 18: 1 1 1 1 1 1
Row 17: 1 1 1 1 1 1
Row 16: 1 1 1 1 1 1
Row 15: 1 1 1 1 1 1
Row 14: 1 1 1 1 1 1
Row 13: 1 1 1 1 1 1
Row 12: 1 1 1 1 1 1
Row 11: 1 1 1 1 1 1
Row 10: 1 1 1 1 1 1
Row 9: 1 1 1 1 1 1
Row 8: 1 1 1 1 1 1
Row 7: 1 1 1 1 1 1
Row 6: 1 1 1 1 1 1 1 1 1 1 1 1 1 1 1 1 1 1 1
Row 5: 1 1 1 1 1 1 1 1 1 1 1 1 1 1 1 1 1 1 1
Row 4: 1 1 1 1 1 1 1 1 1 1 1 1 1 1 1 1 1 1 1
Row 3: 1 1 1 1 1 1 1 1 1 1 1 1 1 1 1 1 1 1 1
Row 2: 1 1 1 1 1 1 1 1 1 1 1 1 1 1 1 1 1 1 1
Row 1: 1 1 1 1 1 1 1 1 1 1 1 1 1 1 1 1 1 1 1

Row 28				
Row 27				
Row 26				
Row 25				
Row 24				
Row 23				
Row 22				
Row 21				
Row 20				
Row 19				
Row 18				
Row 17				
Row 16				
Row 15				
Row 14				
Row 13				
Row 12				
Row 11				
Row 10				
Row 9				
Row 8				
Row 7				
Row 6				
Row 5				
Row 4				
Row 3				
Row 2				
Row 1	✓			

Knitting chart grid (18 columns):

Row	1	2	3	4	5	6	7	8	9	10	11	12	13	14	15	16	17	18
Row 28	m	m	m													m	m	m
Row 27	m	m	m													m	m	m
Row 26	m	m	m	m											m	m	m	m
Row 25	m	m	m	m											m	m	m	m
Row 24	m	m	m	m	m									m	m	m	m	m
Row 23	m	m	m	m	m									m	m	m	m	m
Row 22	m	m	m	m	m	m								m	m	m	m	m
Row 21	m	m	m	m	m	m								m	m	m	m	m
Row 20	m	m	m	m	m	m	m					m	m	m	m	m	m	m
Row 19	m	m	m	m	m	m	m					m	m	m	m	m	m	m
Row 18	m	m	m	m	m	m	m	m			m	m	m	m	m	m	m	m
Row 17	m	m	m	m	m	m	m	m	m		m	m	m	m	m	m	m	m
Row 16	m	m	m	m	m	m	m	m	m		m	m	m	m	m	m	m	m
Row 15	m	m	m	m	m	m	m	m	m	m	m	m	m	m	m	m	m	m
Row 14	m	m	m	m	m	m		m	m	m	m	m	m	m	m	m	m	m
Row 13	m	m	m	m	m	m			m	m	m	m	m	m	m	m	m	m
Row 12	m	m	m	m	m	m			m	m	m	m		m	m	m	m	m
Row 11	m	m	m	m	m	m			m	m	m	m		m	m	m	m	m
Row 10	m	m	m	m	m	m			m	m				m	m	m	m	m
Row 9	m	m	m	m	m	m			m	m				m	m	m	m	m
Row 8	m	m	m	m	m	m								m	m	m	m	m
Row 7	m	m	m	m	m	m								m	m	m	m	m
Row 6	m	m	m	m	m	m								m	m	m	m	m
Row 5	m	m	m	m	m	m								m	m	m	m	m
Row 4	m	m	m	m	m	m								m	m	m	m	m
Row 3	m	m	m	m	m	m								m	m	m	m	m
Row 2	m	m	m	m	m	m							m	m	m	m	m	m
Row 1	m	m	m	m	m	m							m	m	m	m	m	m

Row 28				
Row 27				
Row 26				
Row 25				
Row 24				
Row 23				
Row 22				
Row 21				
Row 20				
Row 19				
Row 18				
Row 17				
Row 16				
Row 15				
Row 14				
Row 13				
Row 12				
Row 11				
Row 10				
Row 9				
Row 8				
Row 7				
Row 6				
Row 5				
Row 4				
Row 3				
Row 2				
Row 1	✓			

	1	2	3	4	5	6	7	8	9	10	11	12	13	14	15	16	17	18
Row 28	n	n	n										n	n	n	n	n	n
Row 27	n	n	n										n	n	n	n	n	n
Row 26	n	n	n										n	n	n	n	n	n
Row 25	n	n	n										n	n	n	n	n	n
Row 24	n	n	n	n									n	n	n	n	n	n
Row 23	n	n	n	n									n	n	n	n	n	n
Row 22	n	n	n	n	n								n	n	n	n	n	n
Row 21	n	n	n	n	n								n	n	n	n	n	n
Row 20	n	n	n	n	n	n							n	n	n	n	n	n
Row 19	n	n	n	n	n	n							n	n	n	n	n	n
Row 18	n	n	n	n	n	n	n						n	n	n	n	n	n
Row 17	n	n	n	n	n	n	n						n	n	n	n	n	n
Row 16	n	n	n	n	n	n	n	n					n	n	n	n	n	n
Row 15	n	n	n	n	n	n	n	n					n	n	n	n	n	n
Row 14	n	n	n	n	n	n	n	n	n				n	n	n	n	n	n
Row 13	n	n	n	n	n	n	n	n	n	n			n	n	n	n	n	n
Row 12	n	n	n	n	n	n	n	n	n	n	n		n	n	n	n	n	n
Row 11	n	n	n	n	n		n	n	n	n	n	n	n	n	n	n	n	n
Row 10	n	n	n	n	n			n	n	n	n	n	n	n	n	n	n	n
Row 9	n	n	n	n	n			n	n	n	n	n	n	n	n	n	n	n
Row 8	n	n	n	n	n			n	n	n	n	n	n	n	n	n	n	n
Row 7	n	n	n	n	n				n	n	n	n	n	n	n	n	n	n
Row 6	n	n	n	n	n					n	n	n	n	n	n	n	n	n
Row 5	n	n	n	n	n						n	n	n	n	n	n	n	n
Row 4	n	n	n	n	n								n	n	n	n	n	n
Row 3	n	n	n	n	n									n	n	n	n	n
Row 2	n	n	n	n	n										n	n	n	n
Row 1	n	n	n	n	n											n	n	n

Row 28				
Row 27				
Row 26				
Row 25				
Row 24				
Row 23				
Row 22				
Row 21				
Row 20				
Row 19				
Row 18				
Row 17				
Row 16				
Row 15				
Row 14				
Row 13				
Row 12				
Row 11				
Row 10				
Row 9				
Row 8				
Row 7				
Row 6				
Row 5				
Row 4				
Row 3				
Row 2	✓			
Row 1	✓			

Letter grid:

		o	o	o	o	o	o	o	o	o	o	o	o	o	o	o	o		
	o	o	o	o	o	o	o	o	o	o	o	o	o	o	o	o	o	o	
o	o	o	o	o	o	o	o	o	o	o	o	o	o	o	o	o	o	o	o	o
o	o	o	o	o	o	o	o	o	o	o	o	o	o	o	o	o	o	o	o	o
o	o	o	o	o	o	o	o	o	o	o	o	o	o	o	o	o	o	o	o	o
o	o	o	o	o	o	o	o	o	o	o	o	o	o	o	o	o	o	o	o	o
o	o	o	o	o	o	o					o	o	o	o	o	o	o			
o	o	o	o	o	o							o	o	o	o	o	o			
o	o	o	o	o	o							o	o	o	o	o	o			
o	o	o	o	o	o							o	o	o	o	o	o			
o	o	o	o	o	o							o	o	o	o	o	o			
o	o	o	o	o	o							o	o	o	o	o	o			
o	o	o	o	o	o							o	o	o	o	o	o			
o	o	o	o	o	o							o	o	o	o	o	o			
o	o	o	o	o	o							o	o	o	o	o	o			
o	o	o	o	o	o							o	o	o	o	o	o			
o	o	o	o	o	o							o	o	o	o	o	o			
o	o	o	o	o	o							o	o	o	o	o	o			
o	o	o	o	o	o							o	o	o	o	o	o			
o	o	o	o	o	o							o	o	o	o	o	o			
o	o	o	o	o	o							o	o	o	o	o	o			
o	o	o	o	o	o	o					o	o	o	o	o	o	o			
o	o	o	o	o	o	o	o	o	o	o	o	o	o	o	o	o	o	o	o	o
o	o	o	o	o	o	o	o	o	o	o	o	o	o	o	o	o	o	o	o	o
o	o	o	o	o	o	o	o	o	o	o	o	o	o	o	o	o	o	o	o	o
o	o	o	o	o	o	o	o	o	o	o	o	o	o	o	o	o	o	o	o	o
	o	o	o	o	o	o	o	o	o	o	o	o	o	o	o	o	o	o	o	
		o	o	o	o	o	o	o	o	o	o	o	o	o	o	o	o			

Row 28				
Row 27				
Row 26				
Row 25				
Row 24				
Row 23				
Row 22				
Row 21				
Row 20				
Row 19				
Row 18				
Row 17				
Row 16				
Row 15				
Row 14				
Row 13				
Row 12				
Row 11				
Row 10				
Row 9				
Row 8				
Row 7				
Row 6				
Row 5				
Row 4				
Row 3				
Row 2				
Row 1	✓			

Right-hand chart (p = purl):

Row	1	2	3	4	5	6	7	8	9	10	11	12	13	14	15	16	17	18	19	20	21	22
28	p	p	p	p	p	p	p	p	p	p	p	p	p	p	p	p	p	p				
27	p	p	p	p	p	p	p	p	p	p	p	p	p	p	p	p	p	p	p			
26	p	p	p	p	p	p	p	p	p	p	p	p	p	p	p	p	p	p	p	p		
25	p	p	p	p	p	p	p	p	p	p	p	p	p	p	p	p	p	p	p	p	p	p
24	p	p	p	p	p	p	p	p	p	p	p	p	p	p	p	p	p	p	p	p	p	
23	p	p	p	p	p	p							p	p	p	p	p	p	p	p		
22	p	p	p	p	p	p								p	p	p	p	p	p	p		
21	p	p	p	p	p	p								p	p	p	p	p	p	p		
20	p	p	p	p	p	p								p	p	p	p	p	p	p		
19	p	p	p	p	p	p								p	p	p	p	p	p	p		
18	p	p	p	p	p	p							p	p	p	p	p	p	p	p		
17	p	p	p	p	p	p						p	p	p	p	p	p	p	p	p		
16	p	p	p	p	p	p	p	p	p	p	p	p	p	p	p	p	p	p	p			
15	p	p	p	p	p	p	p	p	p	p	p	p	p	p	p	p	p	p				
14	p	p	p	p	p	p	p	p	p	p	p	p	p	p	p	p	p					
13	p	p	p	p	p	p	p	p	p	p	p	p	p	p	p	p						
12	p	p	p	p	p	p																
11	p	p	p	p	p	p																
10	p	p	p	p	p	p																
9	p	p	p	p	p	p																
8	p	p	p	p	p	p																
7	p	p	p	p	p	p																
6	p	p	p	p	p	p																
5	p	p	p	p	p	p																
4	p	p	p	p	p	p																
3	p	p	p	p	p	p																
2	p	p	p	p	p	p																
1	p	p	p	p	p	p																

Row 28			
Row 27			
Row 26			
Row 25			
Row 24			
Row 23			
Row 22			
Row 21			
Row 20			
Row 19			
Row 18			
Row 17			
Row 16			
Row 15			
Row 14			
Row 13			
Row 12			
Row 11			
Row 10			
Row 9			
Row 8			
Row 7			
Row 6			
Row 5			
Row 4			
Row 3			
Row 2			
Row 1	✓		

Row 28: q q q q q q q q q q q q q q q q
Row 27: q q q q q q q q q q q q q q q q q
Row 26: q q q q q q q q q q q q q q q q q q q
Row 25: q q q q q q q q q q q q q q q q q q q
Row 24: q q q q q q q q q q q q q q q q q q q
Row 23: q q q q q q q q q q q q q q q q q q q
Row 22: q q q q q q q q   q q q q q q
Row 21: q q q q q q   q q q q q q
Row 20: q q q q q q   q q q q q q
Row 19: q q q q q q   q q q q q q
Row 18: q q q q q q   q q q q q q
Row 17: q q q q q q   q q q q q q
Row 16: q q q q q q   q q q q q q
Row 15: q q q q q q   q q q q q q
Row 14: q q q q q q   q q q q q q
Row 13: q q q q q q   q q q q q q
Row 12: q q q q q q   q q q q q q
Row 11: q q q q q q   q q q q   q q q q q q
Row 10: q q q q q q   q q q q   q q q q q q
Row 9: q q q q q q   q q q q   q q q q q q
Row 8: q q q q q q   q q q q q q q q q q
Row 7: q q q q q q q   q q q q q q q q q q
Row 6: q q q q q q q q q q q q q q q q q q
Row 5: q q q q q q q q q q q q q q q q q q q
Row 4: q q q q q q q q q q q q q q q q q q q
Row 3: q q q q q q q q q q q q q q q q q q q q
Row 2: q q q q q q q q q q q q q q q q q q
Row 1: q q q q q q q q q q q q q q q q q

Row 28				
Row 27				
Row 26				
Row 25				
Row 24				
Row 23				
Row 22				
Row 21				
Row 20				
Row 19				
Row 18				
Row 17				
Row 16				
Row 15				
Row 14				
Row 13				
Row 12				
Row 11				
Row 10				
Row 9				
Row 8				
Row 7				
Row 6				
Row 5				
Row 4				
Row 3				
Row 2				
Row 1	✓			

Letter grid (reading bottom to top, Row 1 to Row 28):

Row 28: r r r r r r r r r r r r r r r r r
Row 27: r r r r r r r r r r r r r r r r r r
Row 26: r r r r r r r r r r r r r r r r r r r
Row 25: r r r r r r r r r r r r r r r r r r r r
Row 24: r r r r r r r r r r r r r r r r r r r r
Row 23: r r r r r r r r r r r r r r
Row 22: r r r r r r r r r r r r r
Row 21: r r r r r r r r r r r r r
Row 20: r r r r r r r r r r r r r
Row 19: r r r r r r r r r r r r r
Row 18: r r r r r r r r r r r r r
Row 17: r r r r r r r r r r r r r r r
Row 16: r r r r r r r r r r r r r r r r r r r r
Row 15: r r r r r r r r r r r r r r r r r r r
Row 14: r r r r r r r r r r r r r r r r r r
Row 13: r r r r r r r r r r r r r r r r r r
Row 12: r r r r r r r r r r
Row 11: r r r r r r r r r r r
Row 10: r r r r r r r r r r r
Row 9: r r r r r r r r r r r r
Row 8: r r r r r r r r r r r r
Row 7: r r r r r r r r r r r
Row 6: r r r r r r r r r r r r
Row 5: r r r r r r r r r r r r
Row 4: r r r r r r r r r r r r
Row 3: r r r r r r r r r r r r
Row 2: r r r r r r r r r r r
Row 1: r r r r r r r r r r

Left chart:

Row 28				
Row 27				
Row 26				
Row 25				
Row 24				
Row 23				
Row 22				
Row 21				
Row 20				
Row 19				
Row 18				
Row 17				
Row 16				
Row 15				
Row 14				
Row 13				
Row 12				
Row 11				
Row 10				
Row 9				
Row 8				
Row 7				
Row 6				
Row 5				
Row 4				
Row 3				
Row 2				
Row 1	✓			

Right chart:

1	2	3	4	5	6	7	8	9	10	11	12	13	14	15	16	17	18	19	20	21	22
		s	s	s	s	s	s	s	s	s	s	s	s	s	s	s	s	s			
	s	s	s	s	s	s	s	s	s	s	s	s	s	s	s	s	s	s	s		
s	s	s	s	s	s	s	s	s	s	s	s	s	s	s	s	s	s	s	s	s	s
s	s	s	s	s	s	s	s	s	s	s	s	s	s	s	s	s	s	s	s	s	s
s	s	s	s	s	s	s	s	s	s	s	s	s	s	s	s	s	s	s	s	s	s
s	s	s	s	s	s	s	s	s	s	s	s	s	s	s	s	s	s	s	s	s	s
s	s	s	s	s	s	s									s	s	s	s	s	s	s
s	s	s	s	s	s										s	s	s	s	s	s	s
s	s	s	s	s											s	s	s	s	s	s	s
s	s	s	s	s											s	s	s	s	s	s	s
s	s	s	s	s											s	s	s	s	s	s	s
s	s	s	s	s	s																
	s	s	s	s	s	s	s	s													
	s	s	s	s	s	s	s	s	s	s	s	s	s								
		s	s	s	s	s	s	s	s	s	s	s	s	s							
						s	s	s	s	s	s	s	s	s							
								s	s	s	s	s	s								
s	s	s	s	s											s	s	s	s	s		
s	s	s	s	s											s	s	s	s	s		
s	s	s	s	s											s	s	s	s	s		
s	s	s	s	s	s									s	s	s	s	s	s		
s	s	s	s	s	s	s							s	s	s	s	s	s	s		
s	s	s	s	s	s	s	s	s	s	s	s	s	s	s	s	s	s	s	s	s	
s	s	s	s	s	s	s	s	s	s	s	s	s	s	s	s	s	s	s	s	s	s
s	s	s	s	s	s	s	s	s	s	s	s	s	s	s	s	s	s	s	s	s	s
s	s	s	s	s	s	s	s	s	s	s	s	s	s	s	s	s	s	s	s	s	s
	s	s	s	s	s	s	s	s	s	s	s	s	s	s	s	s	s	s	s	s	
	s	s	s	s	s	s	s	s	s	s	s	s	s	s	s	s	s	s			

Row 28				
Row 27				
Row 26				
Row 25				
Row 24				
Row 23				
Row 22				
Row 21				
Row 20				
Row 19				
Row 18				
Row 17				
Row 16				
Row 15				
Row 14				
Row 13				
Row 12				
Row 11				
Row 10				
Row 9				
Row 8				
Row 7				
Row 6				
Row 5				
Row 4				
Row 3				
Row 2				
Row 1	✓			

```
t t t t t t t t t t t t t t t t t t t t t t
t t t t t t t t t t t t t t t t t t t t t t
t t t t t t t t t t t t t t t t t t t t t t
t t t t t t t t t t t t t t t t t t t t t t
t t t t t t t t t t t t t t t t t t t t t t
t t t t t t t t t t t t t t t t t t t t t t
                  t t t t t t
                  t t t t t t
                  t t t t t t
                  t t t t t t
                  t t t t t t
                  t t t t t t
                  t t t t t t
                  t t t t t t
                  t t t t t t
                  t t t t t t
                  t t t t t t
                  t t t t t t
                  t t t t t t
                  t t t t t t
                  t t t t t t
                  t t t t t t
                  t t t t t t
                  t t t t t t
                  t t t t t t
                  t t t t t t
                  t t t t t t
                  t t t t t t
```

Row 28				
Row 27				
Row 26				
Row 25				
Row 24				
Row 23				
Row 22				
Row 21				
Row 20				
Row 19				
Row 18				
Row 17				
Row 16				
Row 15				
Row 14				
Row 13				
Row 12				
Row 11				
Row 10				
Row 9				
Row 8				
Row 7				
Row 6				
Row 5				
Row 4				
Row 3				
Row 2				
Row 1	✓			

1	2	3	4	5	6	7	8	9	10	11	12	13	14	15	16	17	18	19	20
u	u	u	u	u	u									u	u	u	u	u	u
u	u	u	u	u	u									u	u	u	u	u	u
u	u	u	u	u	u									u	u	u	u	u	u
u	u	u	u	u	u									u	u	u	u	u	u
u	u	u	u	u	u									u	u	u	u	u	u
u	u	u	u	u	u									u	u	u	u	u	u
u	u	u	u	u	u									u	u	u	u	u	u
u	u	u	u	u	u									u	u	u	u	u	u
u	u	u	u	u	u									u	u	u	u	u	u
u	u	u	u	u	u									u	u	u	u	u	u
u	u	u	u	u	u									u	u	u	u	u	u
u	u	u	u	u	u									u	u	u	u	u	u
u	u	u	u	u	u									u	u	u	u	u	u
u	u	u	u	u	u									u	u	u	u	u	u
u	u	u	u	u	u									u	u	u	u	u	u
u	u	u	u	u	u									u	u	u	u	u	u
u	u	u	u	u	u									u	u	u	u	u	u
u	u	u	u	u	u									u	u	u	u	u	u
u	u	u	u	u	u									u	u	u	u	u	u
u	u	u	u	u	u									u	u	u	u	u	u
u	u	u	u	u	u									u	u	u	u	u	u
u	u	u	u	u	u	u							u	u	u	u	u	u	u
u	u	u	u	u	u	u	u	u	u	u	u	u	u	u	u	u	u	u	u
u	u	u	u	u	u	u	u	u	u	u	u	u	u	u	u	u	u	u	u
u	u	u	u	u	u	u	u	u	u	u	u	u	u	u	u	u	u	u	u
u	u	u	u	u	u	u	u	u	u	u	u	u	u	u	u	u	u	u	u
	u	u	u	u	u	u	u	u	u	u	u	u	u	u	u	u	u	u	u
		u	u	u	u	u	u	u	u	u	u	u	u	u	u	u	u	u	

Row 28				
Row 27				
Row 26				
Row 25				
Row 24				
Row 23				
Row 22				
Row 21				
Row 20				
Row 19				
Row 18				
Row 17				
Row 16				
Row 15				
Row 14				
Row 13				
Row 12				
Row 11				
Row 10				
Row 9				
Row 8				
Row 7				
Row 6				
Row 5				
Row 4				
Row 3				
Row 2				
Row 1	✓			

1	2	3	4	5	6	7	8	9	10	11	12	13	14	15	16	17	18
v	v	v													v	v	v
v	v	v													v	v	v
v	v	v													v	v	v
v	v	v													v	v	v
	v	v	v											v	v	v	
	v	v	v											v	v	v	
	v	v	v											v	v	v	
	v	v	v											v	v	v	
		v	v	v	v							v	v	v	v		
		v	v	v	v							v	v	v	v		
		v	v	v	v							v	v	v	v		
		v	v	v	v							v	v	v	v		
			v	v	v	v	v				v	v	v	v	v		
			v	v	v	v	v				v	v	v	v	v		
			v	v	v	v	v				v	v	v	v	v		
			v	v	v	v	v				v	v	v	v	v		
				v	v	v	v	v		v	v	v	v	v			
				v	v	v	v	v		v	v	v	v	v			
				v	v	v	v	v		v	v	v	v	v			
				v	v	v	v	v		v	v	v	v	v			
				v	v	v	v	v	v	v	v	v	v				
				v	v	v	v	v	v	v	v	v	v				
				v	v	v	v	v	v	v	v	v	v				
				v	v	v	v	v	v	v	v	v	v				
					v	v	v	v	v	v	v	v					
					v	v	v	v	v	v	v	v					
					v	v	v	v	v	v	v	v					
					v	v	v	v	v	v	v	v					

Row 28				
Row 27				
Row 26				
Row 25				
Row 24				
Row 23				
Row 22				
Row 21				
Row 20				
Row 19				
Row 18				
Row 17				
Row 16				
Row 15				
Row 14				
Row 13				
Row 12				
Row 11				
Row 10				
Row 9				
Row 8				
Row 7				
Row 6				
Row 5				
Row 4				
Row 3				
Row 2				
Row 1	✓			

w	w	w	w	w	w									w	w	w	w	w	w
w	w	w	w	w	w									w	w	w	w	w	w
w	w	w	w	w	w									w	w	w	w	w	w
w	w	w	w	w	w									w	w	w	w	w	w
w	w	w	w	w	w									w	w	w	w	w	w
w	w	w	w	w	w									w	w	w	w	w	w
w	w	w	w	w	w									w	w	w	w	w	w
w	w	w	w	w	w									w	w	w	w	w	w
w	w	w	w	w	w				w	w				w	w	w	w	w	w
w	w	w	w	w	w				w	w				w	w	w	w	w	w
w	w	w	w	w	w			w	w	w	w			w	w	w	w	w	w
w	w	w	w	w	w			w	w	w	w			w	w	w	w	w	w
w	w	w	w	w	w		w	w	w	w	w	w		w	w	w	w	w	w
w	w	w	w	w	w		w	w	w	w	w	w		w	w	w	w	w	w
w	w	w	w	w	w	w	w	w	w	w	w	w	w	w	w	w	w	w	w
w	w	w	w	w	w	w	w	w			w	w	w	w	w	w	w	w	w
w	w	w	w	w	w	w	w	w			w	w	w	w	w	w	w	w	w
w	w	w	w	w	w	w	w					w	w	w	w	w	w	w	w
w	w	w	w	w	w	w							w	w	w	w	w	w	w
w	w	w	w	w	w	w							w	w	w	w	w	w	w
w	w	w	w	w	w									w	w	w	w	w	w
w	w	w	w	w	w									w	w	w	w	w	w
w	w	w	w	w											w	w	w	w	w
w	w	w	w	w											w	w	w	w	w
w	w	w	w													w	w	w	w
w	w	w	w													w	w	w	w
w	w	w															w	w	w
w	w	w															w	w	w

Left chart (row tracker):

Row 28				
Row 27				
Row 26				
Row 25				
Row 24				
Row 23				
Row 22				
Row 21				
Row 20				
Row 19				
Row 18				
Row 17				
Row 16				
Row 15				
Row 14				
Row 13				
Row 12				
Row 11				
Row 10				
Row 9				
Row 8				
Row 7				
Row 6				
Row 5				
Row 4				
Row 3				
Row 2				
Row 1	✓			

Right chart (pattern grid, 20 columns):

1	2	3	4	5	6	7	8	9	10	11	12	13	14	15	16	17	18	19	20
x	x	x															x	x	x
x	x	x															x	x	x
x	x	x															x	x	x
	x	x	x													x	x	x	
	x	x	x													x	x	x	
	x	x	x													x	x	x	
		x	x	x											x	x	x		
		x	x	x											x	x	x		
		x	x	x											x	x	x		
		x	x	x	x									x	x	x	x		
			x	x	x	x							x	x	x	x			
				x	x	x	x					x	x	x	x				
				x	x	x	x	x	x	x	x	x	x						
				x	x	x	x	x	x	x	x								
				x	x	x	x	x	x	x	x								
				x	x	x	x	x	x	x	x	x	x						
			x	x	x	x					x	x	x	x					
		x	x	x	x							x	x	x	x				
	x	x	x	x									x	x	x	x			
	x	x	x												x	x	x		
	x	x	x												x	x	x		
	x	x	x												x	x	x		
	x	x	x													x	x	x	
	x	x	x													x	x	x	
	x	x	x													x	x	x	
x	x	x															x	x	x
x	x	x															x	x	x
x	x	x															x	x	x

Row 28			
Row 27			
Row 26			
Row 25			
Row 24			
Row 23			
Row 22			
Row 21			
Row 20			
Row 19			
Row 18			
Row 17			
Row 16			
Row 15			
Row 14			
Row 13			
Row 12			
Row 11			
Row 10			
Row 9			
Row 8			
Row 7			
Row 6			
Row 5			
Row 4			
Row 3			
Row 2			
Row 1	✓		

1	2	3	4	5	6	7	8	9	10	11	12	13	14	15	16	17	18	19	20
y	y	y															y	y	y
y	y	y															y	y	y
y	y	y															y	y	y
	y	y	y													y	y	y	
	y	y	y													y	y	y	
	y	y	y													y	y	y	
		y	y	y											y	y	y		
		y	y	y											y	y	y		
		y	y	y											y	y	y		
		y	y	y	y									y	y	y	y		
			y	y	y	y							y	y	y	y			
				y	y	y	y					y	y	y	y				
					y	y	y	y	y	y	y	y	y	y					
					y	y	y	y	y	y	y	y	y	y					
						y	y	y	y	y	y	y	y						
						y	y	y	y	y	y	y	y						
							y	y	y	y	y	y							
							y	y	y	y	y	y							
							y	y	y	y	y	y							
							y	y	y	y	y	y							
							y	y	y	y	y	y							
							y	y	y	y	y	y							
							y	y	y	y	y	y							
							y	y	y	y	y	y							
							y	y	y	y	y	y							
							y	y	y	y	y	y							
							y	y	y	y	y	y							
							y	y	y	y	y	y							

Row 28				
Row 27				
Row 26				
Row 25				
Row 24				
Row 23				
Row 22				
Row 21				
Row 20				
Row 19				
Row 18				
Row 17				
Row 16				
Row 15				
Row 14				
Row 13				
Row 12				
Row 11				
Row 10				
Row 9				
Row 8				
Row 7				
Row 6				
Row 5				
Row 4				
Row 3				
Row 2	✓			
Row 1	✓			

Row	1	2	3	4	5	6	7	8	9	10	11	12	13	14	15	16	17	18	19	20
Row 28	z	z	z	z	z	z	z	z	z	z	z	z	z	z	z	z	z	z	z	z
Row 27	z	z	z	z	z	z	z	z	z	z	z	z	z	z	z	z	z	z	z	z
Row 26	z	z	z	z	z	z	z	z	z	z	z	z	z	z	z	z	z	z	z	z
Row 25	z	z	z	z	z	z	z	z	z	z	z	z	z	z	z	z	z	z	z	z
Row 24	z	z	z	z	z	z	z	z	z	z	z	z	z	z	z	z	z	z	z	z
Row 23	z	z	z	z	z	z	z	z	z	z	z	z	z	z	z	z	z	z	z	z
Row 22															z	z	z	z	z	z
Row 21															z	z	z	z	z	z
Row 20														z	z	z	z	z	z	
Row 19													z	z	z	z	z	z		
Row 18												z	z	z	z	z	z			
Row 17											z	z	z	z	z	z				
Row 16										z	z	z	z	z	z					
Row 15									z	z	z	z	z	z						
Row 14								z	z	z	z	z	z							
Row 13							z	z	z	z	z	z								
Row 12						z	z	z	z	z	z									
Row 11					z	z	z	z	z	z										
Row 10				z	z	z	z	z	z											
Row 9			z	z	z	z	z	z												
Row 8		z	z	z	z	z	z													
Row 7	z	z	z	z	z	z														
Row 6	z	z	z	z	z	z	z	z	z	z	z	z	z	z	z	z	z	z	z	z
Row 5	z	z	z	z	z	z	z	z	z	z	z	z	z	z	z	z	z	z	z	z
Row 4	z	z	z	z	z	z	z	z	z	z	z	z	z	z	z	z	z	z	z	z
Row 3	z	z	z	z	z	z	z	z	z	z	z	z	z	z	z	z	z	z	z	z
Row 2	z	z	z	z	z	z	z	z	z	z	z	z	z	z	z	z	z	z	z	z
Row 1	z	z	z	z	z	z	z	z	z	z	z	z	z	z	z	z	z	z	z	z

Row 28				
Row 27				
Row 26				
Row 25				
Row 24				
Row 23				
Row 22				
Row 21				
Row 20				
Row 19				
Row 18				
Row 17				
Row 16				
Row 15				
Row 14				
Row 13				
Row 12				
Row 11				
Row 10				
Row 9				
Row 8				
Row 7				
Row 6				
Row 5				
Row 4				
Row 3				
Row 2				
Row 1	✓			

Chart 1 (row tracker, left)

Row 14		
Row 13		
Row 12		
Row 11		
Row 10		
Row 9		
Row 8		
Row 7		
Row 6		
Row 5		
Row 4		
Row 3		
Row 2	✓	
Row 1	✓	

Chart 2 (a, middle top)

				a	a				
				a	a				
			a	a	a	a			
			a	a	a	a			
		a	a			a	a		
		a	a			a	a		
		a	a			a	a		
		a	a	a	a	a	a		
	a	a	a	a	a	a	a	a	
	a	a	a	a	a	a	a	a	
a	a	a	a			a	a	a	a
a	a	a	a			a	a	a	a
a	a	a					a	a	a
a	a	a					a	a	a

Chart 3 (b, right top)

b	b	b	b	b	b	b	b		
b	b	b	b	b	b	b	b	b	
b	b	b	b	b	b	b	b	b	b
b	b	b				b	b	b	b
b	b	b					b	b	b
b	b	b					b	b	
b	b	b	b	b	b	b	b		
b	b	b	b	b	b	b	b		
b	b	b					b	b	
b	b	b					b	b	b
b	b	b				b	b	b	b
b	b	b	b	b	b	b	b	b	b
b	b	b	b	b	b	b	b		
b	b	b	b	b	b	b			

Chart 4 (row tracker, left bottom)

Row 14		
Row 13		
Row 12		
Row 11		
Row 10		
Row 9		
Row 8		
Row 7		
Row 6		
Row 5		
Row 4		
Row 3		
Row 2	✓	
Row 1	✓	

Chart 5 (c, middle bottom)

		c	c	c	c	c	c		
	c	c	c	c	c	c	c	c	
c	c	c	c	c	c	c	c	c	c
c	c	c					c	c	c
c	c	c					c	c	c
c	c	c							
c	c	c							
c	c	c							
c	c	c							
c	c	c					c	c	c
c	c	c					c	c	c
c	c	c	c	c	c	c	c	c	c
	c	c	c	c	c	c	c	c	
		c	c	c	c	c	c		

Chart 6 (d, right bottom)

d	d	d	d	d	d	d	d		
d	d	d	d	d	d	d	d	d	
d	d	d	d	d	d	d	d	d	d
d	d	d				d	d	d	d
d	d	d					d	d	d
d	d	d					d	d	d
d	d	d					d	d	d
d	d	d					d	d	d
d	d	d					d	d	d
d	d	d				d	d	d	d
d	d	d	d	d	d	d	d	d	d
d	d	d	d	d	d	d	d	d	
d	d	d	d	d	d	d	d		

Row 14		
Row 13		
Row 12		
Row 11		
Row 10		
Row 9		
Row 8		
Row 7		
Row 6		
Row 5		
Row 4		
Row 3		
Row 2	✓	
Row 1	✓	

e	e	e	e	e	e	e	e	e	e
e	e	e	e	e	e	e	e	e	
e	e	e	e	e	e	e	e	e	
e	e	e							
e	e	e							
e	e	e	e	e					
e	e	e	e	e					
e	e	e	e	e					
e	e	e	e	e					
e	e	e							
e	e	e							
e	e	e	e	e	e	e	e	e	
e	e	e	e	e	e	e	e	e	
e	e	e	e	e	e	e	e	e	

f	f	f	f	f	f	f	f	f	f
f	f	f	f	f	f	f	f	f	f
f	f	f	f	f	f	f	f	f	f
f	f	f							
f	f	f							
f	f	f							
f	f	f	f	f	f				
f	f	f	f	f	f				
f	f	f	f	f					
f	f	f							
f	f	f							
f	f	f							
f	f	f							
f	f	f							

	g	g	g	g	g	g	g	g	
g	g	g	g	g	g	g	g	g	g
g	g	g	g	g	g	g	g	g	g
g	g	g					g	g	g
g	g	g					g	g	g
g	g	g							
g	g	g							
g	g	g				g	g	g	g
g	g	g				g	g	g	g
g	g	g				g	g	g	
g	g	g				g	g	g	
g	g	g					g	g	g
g	g	g	g	g	g	g	g	g	g
	g	g	g	g	g	g	g	g	

h	h	h					h	h	h
h	h	h					h	h	h
h	h	h					h	h	h
h	h	h					h	h	h
h	h	h					h	h	h
h	h	h	h	h	h	h	h	h	h
h	h	h	h	h	h	h	h	h	h
h	h	h	h	h	h	h	h	h	h
h	h	h	h	h	h	h	h	h	h
h	h	h					h	h	h
h	h	h					h	h	h
h	h	h					h	h	h
h	h	h					h	h	h
h	h	h					h	h	h

Grid 1 (top left)

Row 14		
Row 13		
Row 12		
Row 11		
Row 10		
Row 9		
Row 8		
Row 7		
Row 6		
Row 5		
Row 4		
Row 3		
Row 2		
Row 1	✓	

Grid 2 (top middle — i)

i	i	i	i	i	i	i	i	i	i
i	i	i	i	i	i	i	i	i	
i	i	i	i	i	i	i	i	i	i
			i	i	i	i			
			i	i	i	i			
			i	i	i	i			
			i	i	i	i			
			i	i	i	i			
			i	i	i	i			
			i	i	i	i			
			i	i	i	i			
i	i	i	i	i	i	i	i	i	i
i	i	i	i	i	i	i	i	i	i
i	i	i	i	i	i	i	i	i	i

Grid 3 (top right — j)

j	j	j	j	j	j	j	j	j	j
j	j	j	j	j	j	j	j	j	j
j	j	j	j	j	j	j	j	j	j
j	j	j	j	j	j	j	j	j	j
					j	j	j		
					j	j	j		
					j	j	j		
					j	j	j		
					j	j	j		
j	j	j			j	j	j		
j	j	j			j	j	j		
j	j	j	j	j	j				
j	j	j	j	j	j	j			
	j	j	j	j	j				

Grid 4 (bottom left)

Row 14		
Row 13		
Row 12		
Row 11		
Row 10		
Row 9		
Row 8		
Row 7		
Row 6		
Row 5		
Row 4		
Row 3		
Row 2		
Row 1	✓	

Grid 5 (bottom middle — k)

k	k	k				k	k	k	
k	k	k				k	k	k	
k	k	k			k	k	k		
k	k	k			k	k	k		
k	k	k		k	k	k			
k	k	k	k	k	k	k	k		
k	k	k	k	k	k	k			
k	k	k	k	k	k	k			
k	k	k	k	k	k	k	k		
k	k	k	k	k	k	k	k		
k	k	k			k	k	k		
k	k	k			k	k	k		
k	k	k				k	k	k	
k	k	k				k	k	k	

Grid 6 (bottom right — l)

l	l	l							
l	l	l							
l	l	l							
l	l	l							
l	l	l							
l	l	l							
l	l	l							
l	l	l							
l	l	l							
l	l	l							
l	l	l	l	l	l	l	l	l	l
l	l	l	l	l	l	l	l	l	l
l	l	l	l	l	l	l	l	l	l
l	l	l	l	l	l	l	l	l	l

Top-left row table

Row 14		
Row 13		
Row 12		
Row 11		
Row 10		
Row 9		
Row 8		
Row 7		
Row 6		
Row 5		
Row 4		
Row 3		
Row 2		✓
Row 1	✓	

"m" chart

m	m							m	m
m	m	m					m	m	m
m	m	m					m	m	m
m	m	m	m			m	m	m	m
m	m	m	m			m	m	m	m
m	m	m	m	m	m	m	m	m	m
m	m	m	m	m	m	m	m	m	m
m	m	m		m	m		m	m	m
m	m	m		m	m		m	m	m
m	m	m		m	m		m	m	m
m	m	m		m	m		m	m	m
m	m	m		m	m		m	m	m
m	m	m		m	m		m	m	m
m	m	m		m	m		m	m	m

"n" chart

n	n	n					n	n	n
n	n	n					n	n	n
n	n	n	n				n	n	n
n	n	n	n				n	n	n
n	n	n	n	n			n	n	n
n	n	n	n	n			n	n	n
n	n	n	n	n	n		n	n	n
n	n	n	n	n	n		n	n	n
n	n	n		n	n	n	n	n	n
n	n	n		n	n	n	n	n	n
n	n	n			n	n	n	n	n
n	n	n			n	n	n	n	n
n	n	n					n	n	n
n	n	n					n	n	n

Bottom-left row table

Row 14		
Row 13		
Row 12		
Row 11		
Row 10		
Row 9		
Row 8		
Row 7		
Row 6		
Row 5		
Row 4		
Row 3		
Row 2		✓
Row 1	✓	

"o" chart

	o	o	o	o	o	o				
	o	o	o	o	o	o	o	o		
o	o	o	o	o	o	o	o	o	o	o
o	o	o					o	o	o	
o	o	o					o	o	o	
o	o	o					o	o	o	
o	o	o					o	o	o	
o	o	o					o	o	o	
o	o	o					o	o	o	
o	o	o					o	o	o	
o	o	o	o	o	o	o	o	o	o	
	o	o	o	o	o	o	o	o		
	o	o	o	o	o	o				

"p" chart

p	p	p	p	p	p	p	p		
p	p	p	p	p	p	p	p	p	
p	p	p	p	p	p	p	p	p	p
p	p	p					p	p	p
p	p	p					p	p	p
p	p	p					p	p	p
p	p	p	p	p	p	p	p	p	
p	p	p	p	p	p	p	p		
p	p	p	p	p	p	p			
p	p	p							
p	p	p							
p	p	p							
p	p	p							
p	p	p							

Row label grids (top-left and bottom-left)

Row 14		
Row 13		
Row 12		
Row 11		
Row 10		
Row 9		
Row 8		
Row 7		
Row 6		
Row 5		
Row 4		
Row 3		
Row 2		
Row 1	✓	

Letter q grid (top-middle)

		q	q	q	q	q	q		
	q	q	q	q	q	q	q	q	
q	q	q	q	q	q	q	q	q	q
q	q	q					q	q	q
q	q	q					q	q	q
q	q	q					q	q	q
q	q	q					q	q	q
q	q	q					q	q	q
q	q	q					q	q	q
q	q	q			q		q	q	q
q	q	q				q	q	q	q
q	q	q	q	q	q	q	q	q	q
	q	q	q	q	q	q	q	q	
		q	q	q	q	q	q		

Letter r grid (top-right)

r	r	r	r	r	r	r	r		
r	r	r	r	r	r	r	r	r	
r	r	r	r	r	r	r	r	r	r
r	r	r					r	r	r
r	r	r					r	r	r
r	r	r					r	r	r
r	r	r	r	r	r	r	r		
r	r	r	r	r	r	r	r		
r	r	r	r	r	r				
r	r	r				r	r	r	
r	r	r					r	r	r
r	r	r					r	r	r
r	r	r					r	r	r
r	r	r					r	r	r

Letter s grid (bottom-middle)

		s	s	s	s	s	s		
	s	s	s	s	s	s	s	s	
s	s	s	s	s	s	s	s	s	s
s	s	s	s	s			s	s	s
s	s	s	s				s	s	s
	s	s	s	s			s	s	s
		s	s	s	s				
			s	s	s	s			
			s	s	s	s			
s	s	s			s	s	s	s	
s	s	s				s	s	s	s
s	s	s	s	s	s	s	s	s	s
	s	s	s	s	s	s	s	s	
		s	s	s	s	s	s		

Letter t grid (bottom-right)

t	t	t	t	t	t	t	t	t	
t	t	t	t	t	t	t	t	t	t
t	t	t	t	t	t	t	t	t	t
t	t	t	t	t	t	t	t	t	t
			t	t	t	t			
			t	t	t	t			
			t	t	t	t			
			t	t	t	t			
			t	t	t	t			
			t	t	t	t			
			t	t	t	t			
			t	t	t	t			
			t	t	t	t			
			t	t	t	t			

Row 14		
Row 13		
Row 12		
Row 11		
Row 10		
Row 9		
Row 8		
Row 7		
Row 6		
Row 5		
Row 4		
Row 3		
Row 2		
Row 1	✓	

u	u	u					u	u	u
u	u	u					u	u	u
u	u	u					u	u	u
u	u	u					u	u	u
u	u	u					u	u	u
u	u	u					u	u	u
u	u	u					u	u	u
u	u	u					u	u	u
u	u	u					u	u	u
u	u	u					u	u	u
u	u	u					u	u	u
u	u	u	u	u	u	u	u	u	u
	u	u	u	u	u	u	u	u	
		u	u	u	u	u	u		

v	v							v	v
v	v							v	v
v	v							v	v
v	v							v	v
	v	v					v	v	
	v	v					v	v	
	v	v					v	v	
		v	v			v	v		
		v	v			v	v		
		v	v			v	v		
			v	v	v	v			
			v	v	v	v			
				v	v				
				v	v				

Row 14		
Row 13		
Row 12		
Row 11		
Row 10		
Row 9		
Row 8		
Row 7		
Row 6		
Row 5		
Row 4		
Row 3		
Row 2		
Row 1	✓	

w	w							w	w
w	w							w	w
w	w							w	w
w	w							w	w
w	w							w	w
	w	w		w	w		w	w	
	w	w		w	w		w	w	
	w	w		w	w		w	w	
	w	w		w	w		w	w	
	w	w		w	w		w	w	
		w		w	w		w		
		w	w			w	w		
		w	w			w	w		
		w	w			w	w		

x	x	x					x	x	x
x	x	x					x	x	x
	x	x	x			x	x	x	
	x	x	x			x	x	x	
		x	x			x	x		
		x	x			x	x		
				x	x				
				x	x				
		x	x			x	x		
		x	x			x	x		
	x	x	x			x	x	x	
	x	x	x			x	x	x	
x	x	x					x	x	x
x	x	x					x	x	x

Row 14		
Row 13		
Row 12		
Row 11		
Row 10		
Row 9		
Row 8		
Row 7		
Row 6		
Row 5		
Row 4		
Row 3		
Row 2		
Row 1	✓	

y	y	y				y	y	y
y	y	y				y	y	y
	y	y	y		y	y	y	
	y	y	y		y	y	y	
		y	y		y	y		
		y	y		y	y		
	y	y	y	y	y	y		
		y	y	y	y			
		y	y	y	y			
			y	y				
			y	y				
			y	y				
			y	y				
			y	y				

z	z	z	z	z	z	z	z	z	z
z	z	z	z	z	z	z	z	z	z
z	z	z	z	z	z	z	z	z	z
							z	z	z
						z	z	z	
					z	z	z		
				z	z	z			
			z	z	z				
		z	z	z					
	z	z	z						
z	z	z							
z	z	z	z	z	z	z	z	z	z
z	z	z	z	z	z	z	z	z	z
z	z	z	z	z	z	z	z	z	z

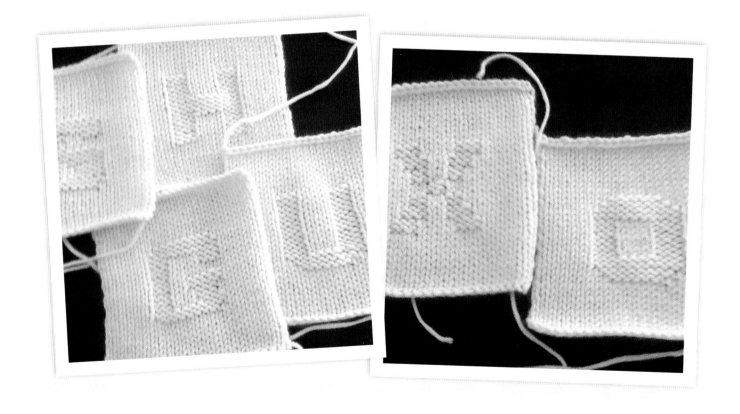

Home Patterns

SINGLE INITIAL
GARTER STITCH PILLOW

Single-Point
Needles

Yarn: Debbie Bliss cashmerino aran,
55% merino wool/33% microfiber/12% cashmere,
100 yds per 50 g

Yards Required: 225

Needles: US 8 (5mm) recommended, but I used US 5 (3.75mm)

Gauge: 18 stitches and 24 rows equal 4 inches

Finished Size: 14 inches tall and 13 inches wide

Abbreviations: K (k): Knit; P (p): Purl

Cast on 82 stitches on a single-point needle.

Row	Stitch Pattern	Done	Row	Stitch Pattern	Done
Outside Border			Row 14	K82	
			Row 15	P82	
Row 1	K82	✓	Row 16	P82	
Row 2	K82		Row 17	K82	
Row 3	P82		Row 18	K82	
Row 4	P82		Row 19	P82	
Row 5	K82		Row 20	P82	
Row 6	K82		Row 21	K82	
Row 7	P82		Row 22	K82	
Row 8	P82		Row 23	P82	
Row 9	K82		Row 24	P82	
Row 10	K82		Row 25	K82	
Row 11	P82		Row 26	K82	
Row 12	P82		Row 27	P82	
Row 13	K82		Row 28	P82	

Inside Border

Row	Stitch Pattern	Done
Row 1	K17, p48, k17	
Row 2	K17, p48, k17	
Row 3	P82	
Row 4	P82	
Row 5	K17, p48, k17	
Row 6	K17, p48, k17	
Row 7	P82	
Row 8	P82	
Row 9	K17, p48, k17	
Row 10	K17, p48, k17	
Row 11	P82	
Row 12	P82	
Row 13	K17, p48, k17	
Row 14	K17, p48, k17	
Row 15	P82	
Row 16	P82	
Row 17	K17, p48, k17	
Row 18	K17, p48, k17	
Row 19	P82	
Row 20	P82	
Row 21	K17, p48, k17	
Row 22	K17, p48, k17	
Row 23	P82	
Row 24	P82	
Row 25	K17, p48, k17	
Row 26	K17, p48, k17	
Row 27	P82	
Row 28	P82	

Below the Letter

Row	Stitch Pattern	Done
Row 1	K82	
Row 2	K17, p48, k17	
Row 3	P17, k48, p17	
Row 4	P82	
Row 5	K82	

Row	Stitch Pattern	Done
Row 6	K17, p48, k17	
Row 7	P17, k48, p17	
Row 8	P82	

The Letter

"Customize 20" refers to the 20 stitches
of the letter you're knitting.

Row	Stitch Pattern	Done
Row 1	K31, *customize* 20, k31	
Row 2	K17, p14, *customize* 20, p14, k17	
Row 3	P17, k14, *customize* 20, k14, p17	
Row 4	P31, *customize* 20, p31	
Row 5	K31, *customize* 20, k31	
Row 6	K17, p14, *customize* 20, p14, k17	
Row 7	P17, k14, *customize* 20, k14, p17	
Row 8	P31, *customize* 20, p31	
Row 9	K31, *customize* 20, k31	
Row 10	K17, p14, *customize* 20, p14, k17	
Row 11	P17, k14, *customize* 20, k14, p17	
Row 12	P31, *customize* 20, p31	
Row 13	K31, *customize* 20, k31	
Row 14	K17, p14, *customize* 20, p14, k17	
Row 15	P17, k14, *customize* 20, k14, p17	
Row 16	P31, *customize* 20, p31	
Row 17	K31, *customize* 20, k31	
Row 18	K17, p14, *customize* 20, p14, k17	
Row 19	P17, k14, *customize* 20, k14, p17	
Row 20	P31, *customize* 20, p31	
Row 21	K31, *customize* 20, k31	
Row 22	K17, p14, *customize* 20, p14, k17	
Row 23	P17, k14, *customize* 20, k14, p17	
Row 24	P31, *customize* 20, p31	
Row 25	K31, *customize* 20, k31	
Row 26	K17, p14, *customize* 20, p14, k17	
Row 27	P17, k14, *customize* 20, k14, p17	
Row 28	P31, *customize* 20, p31	

Row	Stitch Pattern	Done

Above the Letter

Row	Stitch Pattern
Row 1	K82
Row 2	K17, p48, k17
Row 3	P17, k48, p17
Row 4	P82
Row 5	K82
Row 6	K17, p48, k17
Row 7	P17, k48, p17
Row 8	P82

Inside Border

Row	Stitch Pattern
Row 1	K17, p48, k17
Row 2	K17, p48, k17
Row 3	P82
Row 4	P82
Row 5	K17, p48, k17
Row 6	K17, p48, k17
Row 7	P82
Row 8	P82
Row 9	K17, p48, k17
Row 10	K17, p48, k17
Row 11	P82
Row 12	P82
Row 13	K17, p48, k17
Row 14	K17, p48, k17
Row 15	P82
Row 16	P82
Row 17	K17, p48, k17
Row 18	K17, p48, k17
Row 19	P82
Row 20	P82
Row 21	K17, p48, k17
Row 22	K17, p48, k17
Row 23	P82
Row 24	P82

Row	Stitch Pattern	Done
Row 25	K17, p48, k17
Row 26	K17, p48, k17
Row 27	P82
Row 28	P82

Outside Border

Row	Stitch Pattern
Row 1	K82
Row 2	K82
Row 3	P82
Row 4	P82
Row 5	K82
Row 6	K82
Row 7	P82
Row 8	P82
Row 9	K82
Row 10	K82
Row 11	P82
Row 12	P82
Row 13	K82
Row 14	K82
Row 15	P82
Row 16	P82
Row 17	K82
Row 18	K82
Row 19	P82
Row 20	P82
Row 21	K82
Row 22	K82
Row 23	P82
Row 24	P82
Row 25	K82
Row 26	K82
Row 27	P82
Row 28	P82

Cast off 82 stitches and secure loose threads.

FOUR LETTER SIGNATURE PILLOW

Single-Point Needles

Yarn: Debbie Bliss cashmerino aran,
55% merino wool/33% microfiber/12% cashmere,
100 yds per 50g

Yards Required: 225

Needles: US 8 (5mm) recommended, but I used US 5 (3.75mm)

Gauge: 18 stitches and 24 rows equal 4 inches

Finished Size: 12 inches tall and 13 inches wide

Abbreviations: K (k): Knit; P (p): Purl

Cast on 82 stitches on a single-point needle.

Row	*Stitch Pattern*	*Done*

Outside Border

Row	Stitch Pattern	Done
Row 1	K82	✓
Row 2	K82	
Row 3	P82	
Row 4	P82	
Row 5	K82	
Row 6	K82	
Row 7	P82	
Row 8	P82	
Row 9	K82	
Row 10	K82	
Row 11	P82	
Row 12	P82	

Row	*Stitch Pattern*	*Done*

Below the Letters

Row	Stitch Pattern
Row 1	K82
Row 2	K8, p30, k6, p30, k8
Row 3	P8, k30, p6, k30, p8
Row 4	P82
Row 5	K82
Row 6	K8, p30, k6, p30, k8

Row	Stitch Pattern	Done	Row	Stitch Pattern	Done

Lower Letters

"Customize 20" refers to the 20 stitches
of the letter you're knitting.

Row	Stitch Pattern	Done
Row 1	P8, k5, *customize* 20, k5, p6, k5, *customize* 20, k5, p8	
Row 2	P13, *customize* 20, p16, *customize* 20, p13	
Row 3	K13, *customize* 20, k16, *customize* 20, k13	
Row 4	K8, p5, *customize* 20, p5, k6, p5, *customize* 20, p5, k8	
Row 5	P8, k5, *customize* 20, k5, p6, k5, *customize* 20, k5, p8	
Row 6	P13, *customize* 20, p16, *customize* 20, p13	
Row 7	K13, *customize* 20, k16, *customize* 20, k13	
Row 8	K8, p5, *customize* 20, p5, k6, p5, *customize* 20, p5, k8	
Row 9	P8, k5, *customize* 20, k5, p6, k5, *customize* 20, k5, p8	
Row 10	P13, *customize* 20, p16, *customize* 20, p13	
Row 11	K13, *customize* 20, k16, *customize* 20, k13	
Row 12	K8, p5, *customize* 20, p5, k6, p5, *customize* 20, p5, k8	
Row 13	P8, k5, *customize* 20, k5, p6, k5, *customize* 20, k5, p8	
Row 14	P13, *customize* 20, p16, *customize* 20, p13	
Row 15	K13, *customize* 20, k16, *customize* 20, k13	
Row 16	K8, p5, *customize* 20, p5, k6, p5, *customize* 20, p5, k8	
Row 17	P8, k5, *customize* 20, k5, p6, k5, *customize* 20, k5, p8	
Row 18	P13, *customize* 20, p16, *customize* 20, p13	
Row 19	K13, *customize* 20, k16, *customize* 20, k13	
Row 20	K8, p5, *customize* 20, p5, k6, p5, *customize* 20, p5, k8	
Row 21	P8, k5, *customize* 20, k5, p6, k5, *customize* 20, k5, p8	
Row 22	P13, *customize* 20, p16, *customize* 20, p13	
Row 23	K13, *customize* 20, k16, *customize* 20, k13	
Row 24	K8, p5, *customize* 20, p5, k6, p5, *customize* 20, p5, k8	
Row 25	P8, k5, *customize* 20, k5, p6, k5, *customize* 20, k5, p8	
Row 26	P13, *customize* 20, p16, *customize* 20, p13	
Row 27	K13, *customize* 20, k16, *customize* 20, k13	
Row 28	K8, p5, *customize* 20, p5, k6, p5, *customize* 20, p5, k8	

Above the Letters

Row	Stitch Pattern	Done
Row 1	P8, k30, p6, k30, p8	
Row 2	P82	
Row 3	K82	
Row 4	K8, p30, k6, p30, k8	
Row 5	P8, k30, p6, k30, p8	
Row 6	P82	

Mid Section

Row	Stitch Pattern	Done
Row 1	K82	
Row 2	K82	
Row 3	P82	

Row	Stitch Pattern	Done
Row 4	P82	
Row 5	K82	
Row 6	K82	
Row 7	P82	
Row 8	P82	

Below the Letters

Row	Stitch Pattern	Done
Row 1	K82	
Row 2	K8, p30, k6, p30, k8	
Row 3	P8, k30, p6, k30, p8	
Row 4	P82	
Row 5	K82	
Row 6	K8, p30, k6, p30, k8	

Upper Letters

Row	Stitch Pattern	Done
Row 1	P8, k5, *customize* 20, k5, p6, k5, *customize* 20, k5, p8	
Row 2	P13, *customize* 20, p16, *customize* 20, p13	
Row 3	K13, *customize* 20, k16, *customize* 20, k13	
Row 4	K8, p5, *customize* 20, p5, k6, p5, *customize* 20, p5, k8	
Row 5	P8, k5, *customize* 20, k5, p6, k5, *customize* 20, k5, p8	
Row 6	P13, *customize* 20, p16, *customize* 20, p13	
Row 7	K13, *customize* 20, k16, *customize* 20, k13	
Row 8	K8, p5, *customize* 20, p5, k6, p5, *customize* 20, p5, k8	
Row 9	P8, k5, *customize* 20, k5, p6, k5, *customize* 20, k5, p8	
Row 10	P13, *customize* 20, p16, *customize* 20, p13	
Row 11	K13, *customize* 20, k16, *customize* 20, k13	
Row 12	K8, p5, *customize* 20, p5, k6, p5, *customize* 20, p5, k8	
Row 13	P8, k5, *customize* 20, k5, p6, k5, *customize* 20, k5, p8	
Row 14	P13, *customize* 20, p16, *customize* 20, p13	
Row 15	K13, *customize* 20, k16, *customize* 20, k13	
Row 16	K8, p5, *customize* 20, p5, k6, p5, *customize* 20, p5, k8	
Row 17	P8, k5, *customize* 20, k5, p6, k5, *customize* 20, k5, p8	
Row 18	P13, *customize* 20, p16, *customize* 20, p13	
Row 19	K13, *customize* 20, k16, *customize* 20, k13	
Row 20	K8, p5, *customize* 20, p5, k6, p5, *customize* 20, p5, k8	
Row 21	P8, k5, *customize* 20, k5, p6, k5, *customize* 20, k5, p8	
Row 22	P13, *customize* 20, p16, *customize* 20, p13	
Row 23	K13, *customize* 20, k16, *customize* 20, k13	
Row 24	K8, p5, *customize* 20, p5, k6, p5, *customize* 20, p5, k8	
Row 25	P8, k5, *customize* 20, k5, p6, k5, *customize* 20, k5, p8	
Row 26	P13, *customize* 20, p16, *customize* 20, p13	
Row 27	K13, *customize* 20, k16, *customize* 20, k13	
Row 28	K8, p5, *customize* 20, p5, k6, p5, *customize* 20, p5, k8	

Above the Letters

Row		
Row 1	P8, k30, p6, k30, p8	
Row 2	P82	
Row 3	K82	
Row 4	K8, p30, k6, p30, k8	
Row 5	P8, k30, p6, k30, p8	
Row 6	P82	

Outside Border

Row		
Row 1	K82	
Row 2	K82	
Row 3	P82	
Row 4	P82	
Row 5	K82	
Row 6	K82	
Row 7	P82	
Row 8	P82	
Row 9	K82	
Row 10	K82	
Row 11	P82	
Row 12	P82	

Cast off 82 stitches and secure loose threads.

HOW TO MAKE A PILLOW COVER

The preceding pages presented several patterns for knitting personalized pillow fronts. Here's how to assemble them with fabric to cover a pillow form.

> Press and block your knitted piece noting final dimensions.

> Cut a piece of iron-on stabilizer to the pillow dimensions and attach to the back of knitted piece.

> Cut a piece of decorative fabric to the same dimensions as the backed pillow piece.

> Attach decorative trim or cording to the right side of the fabric approximately ⅜" from outer edge. This is optional.

> Put right sides of knitted piece and fabric piece together and sew three sides of the square with a ⅜" seam allowance.

> Sew the fourth side just beyond the corner turn, allowing a large opening to insert the pillow form.

> Turn the cover inside-out and smooth the surface.

> Insert the pillow form and adjust to straighten.

> Hand-sew remaining opening closed.

> That's it!

FAMILY CREST PILLOW

Single-Point Needles

Yarn: Debbie Bliss cashmerino aran,
55% merino wool/33% microfiber/12%
cashmere, 100 yds per 50g

Yards Required: 250

Needles: US 8 (5mm) recommended, but I used US 5 (3.75mm)

Gauge: 18 stitches and 24 rows equal 4 inches

Finished Size: 12 inches tall and 14 inches wide

Abbreviations: K (k): Knit; P (p): Purl

Cast on 88 stitches on a single-point needle.

Row	Stitch Pattern	Done	Row	Stitch Pattern	Done
Lower Background			Row 13	K88	
			Row 14	P88	
Row 1	K88	✓	Row 15	K88	
Row 2	P88		Row 16	P88	
Row 3	K88		Row 17	K88	
Row 4	P88		Row 18	P88	
Row 5	K88		Row 19	K88	
Row 6	P88		Row 20	P88	
Row 7	K88		Row 21	K88	
Row 8	P88		Row 22	P88	
Row 9	K88		Row 23	K88	
Row 10	P88		Row 24	P88	
Row 11	K88		Row 25	K88	
Row 12	P88		Row 26	P88	

Bottom of Shield

Row	Stitch Pattern	Done
Row 1	K88	
Row 2	P37, k6, p2, k6, p37	
Row 3	K36, p16, k36	
Row 4	P32, k24, p32	
Row 5	K29, p30, k29	
Row 6	P28, k32, p28	
Row 7	K28, p32, k28	
Row 8	P28, k32, p28	
Row 9	K28, p32, k28	

Letter

"Customize 20" refers to the 20 stitches
of the letter you're knitting

Row	Stitch Pattern	Done
Row 1	P28, k6, *customize* 20, k6, p28	
Row 2	K28, p6, *customize* 20, p6, k28	
Row 3	P27, k7, *customize* 20, k7, p27	
Row 4	K27, p7, *customize* 20, p7, k27	
Row 5	P27, k7, *customize* 20, k7, p27	
Row 6	K27, p7, *customize* 20, p7, k27	
Row 7	P27, k7, *customize* 20, k7, p27	
Row 8	K27, p7, *customize* 20, p7, k27	
Row 9	P27, k7, *customize* 20, k7, p27	
Row 10	K27, p7, *customize* 20, p7, k27	
Row 11	P26, k8, *customize* 20, k8, p26	
Row 12	K26, p8, *customize* 20, p8, k26	
Row 13	P26, k8, *customize* 20, k8, p26	
Row 14	K26, p8, *customize* 20, p8, k26	
Row 15	P26, k8, *customize* 20, k8, p26	
Row 16	K26, p8, *customize* 20, p8, k26	
Row 17	P26, k8, *customize* 20, k8, p26	
Row 18	K26, p8, *customize* 20, p8, k26	
Row 19	P25, k9, *customize* 20, k9, p25	
Row 20	K25, p9, *customize* 20, p9, k25	
Row 21	P25, k9, *customize* 20, k9, p25	
Row 22	K25, p9, *customize* 20, p9, k25	
Row 23	P25, k9, *customize* 20, k9, p25	
Row 24	K25, p9, *customize* 20, p9, k25	
Row 25	P25, k9, *customize* 20, k9, p25	
Row 26	K25, p9, *customize* 20, p9, k25	
Row 27	P24, k10, *customize* 20, k10, p24	
Row 28	K24, p10, *customize* 20, p10, k24	

Top of Shield

Row	Stitch Pattern	Done
Row 1	P24, k40, p24	
Row 2	K24, p40, k24	
Row 3	P24, k40, p24	
Row 4	K24, p40, k24	
Row 5	P24, k40, p24	
Row 6	K24, p40, k24	
Row 7	P23, k42, p23	
Row 8	K23, p42, k23	
Row 9	P23, k42, p23	
Row 10	K23, p42, k23	
Row 11	P23, k42, p23	
Row 12	K23, p42, k23	
Row 13	P23, k42, p23	
Row 14	K22, p44, k22	
Row 15	P22, k44, p22	
Row 16	K26, p6, k9, p6, k9, p6, k26	
Row 17	P26, k6, p9, k6, p9, k6, p26	
Row 18	K27, p4, k11, p4, k11, p4, k27	
Row 19	P27, k4, p11, k4, p11, k4, p27	
Row 20	K28, p2, k13, p2, k13, p2, k28	
Row 21	P28, k2, p13, k2, p13, k2, p28	

Upper Background

Row	Stitch Pattern	Done
Row 1	K88	
Row 2	P88	
Row 3	K88	

Row	Stitch Pattern	Done		Row	Stitch Pattern	Done
Row 4	P88			Row 17	K88	
Row 5	K88			Row 18	P88	
Row 6	P88			Row 19	K88	
Row 7	K88.			Row 20	P88	
Row 8	P88			Row 21	K88	
Row 9	K88			Row 22	P88	
Row 10	P88			Row 23	K88	
Row 11	K88			Row 24	P88	
Row 12	P88			Row 25	K88	
Row 13	K88			Row 26	P88	
Row 14	P88					
Row 15	K88					
Row 16	P88					

Cast off 88 stitches and secure loose threads.

An iron-on stabilizer on the back of the knitted crest allows for a more polished look and also makes assembly easier.

A self-welt piping is a great finishing technique. It is simple and elegant and allows the knitted crest to be the

TIC TAC TOE PILLOW

Single-Point Needles

Yarn: Debbie Bliss cashmerino aran,
55% merino wool/33% microfiber/12% cashmere,
100 yds per 50g

Yards Required: 250

Needles: US 8 (5mm) recommended, but I used US 5 (3.75mm)

Gauge: 18 stitches and 24 rows equal 4 inches

Finished Size: 12 inches tall and 13 inches wide

Abbreviations: K (k): Knit; P (p): Purl

Cast on 90 stitches on a single-point needle.

Row	Stitch Pattern	Done

Outside Border

Row	Stitch Pattern	Done
Row 1	P30, k30, p30	✓
Row 2	K30, p30, k30	
Row 3	P30, k30, p30	
Row 4	K30, p30, k30	
Row 5	P30, k30, p30	
Row 6	K30, p30, k30	
Row 7	P30, k30, p30	
Row 8	K30, p30, k30	

Bottom Three Letters

"Customize 20" refers to the 20 stitches of the letter you're knitting.

Row	Stitch Pattern	Done
Row 1	K5, *customize* 20, k5, p5, *customize* 20, p5, k5, *customize* 20, k5	
Row 2	P5, *customize* 20, p5, k5, *customize* 20, k5, p5, *customize* 20, p5	
Row 3	K5, *customize* 20, k5, p5, *customize* 20, p5, k5, *customize* 20, k5	

Row	Stitch Pattern	Done	Row	Stitch Pattern	Done
Row 4	P5, *customize* 20, p5, k5, *customize* 20, k5, p5, *customize* 20, p5		Row 17	K5, *customize* 20, k5, p5, *customize* 20, p5, k5, *customize* 20, k5	
Row 5	K5, *customize* 20, k5, p5, *customize* 20, p5, k5, *customize* 20, k5		Row 18	P5, *customize* 20, p5, k5, *customize* 20, k5, p5, *customize* 20, p5	
Row 6	P5, *customize* 20, p5, k5, *customize* 20, k5, p5, *customize* 20, p5		Row 19	K5, *customize* 20, k5, p5, *customize* 20, p5, k5, *customize* 20, k5	
Row 7	K5, *customize* 20, k5, p5, *customize* 20, p5, k5, *customize* 20, k5		Row 20	P5, *customize* 20, p5, k5, *customize* 20, k5, p5, *customize* 20, p5	
Row 8	P5, *customize* 20, p5, k5, *customize* 20, k5, p5, *customize* 20, p5		Row 21	K5, *customize* 20, k5, p5, *customize* 20, p5, k5, *customize* 20, k5	
Row 9	K5, *customize* 20, k5, p5, *customize* 20, p5, k5, *customize* 20, k5		Row 22	P5, *customize* 20, p5, k5, *customize* 20, k5, p5, *customize* 20, p5	
Row 10	P5, *customize* 20, p5, k5, *customize* 20, k5, p5, *customize* 20, p5		Row 23	K5, *customize* 20, k5, p5, *customize* 20, p5, k5, *customize* 20, k5	
Row 11	K5, *customize* 20, k5, p5, *customize* 20, p5, k5, *customize* 20, k5		Row 24	P5, *customize* 20, p5, k5, *customize* 20, k5, p5, *customize* 20, p5	
Row 12	P5, *customize* 20, p5, k5, *customize* 20, k5, p5, *customize* 20, p5		Row 25	K5, *customize* 20, k5, p5, *customize* 20, p5, k5, *customize* 20, k5	
Row 13	K5, *customize* 20, k5, p5, *customize* 20, p5, k5, *customize* 20, k5		Row 26	P5, *customize* 20, p5, k5, *customize* 20, k5, p5, *customize* 20, p5	
Row 14	P5, *customize* 20, p5, k5, *customize* 20, k5, p5, *customize* 20, p5		Row 27	K5, *customize* 20, k5, p5, *customize* 20, p5, k5, *customize* 20, k5	
Row 15	K5, *customize* 20, k5, p5, *customize* 20, p5, k5, *customize* 20, k5		Row 28	P5, *customize* 20, p5, k5, *customize* 20, k5, p5, *customize* 20, p5	
Row 16	P5, *customize* 20, p5, k5, *customize* 20, k5, p5, *customize* 20, p5				

Row	Stitch Pattern	Done	Row	Stitch Pattern	Done

Lower Transition

Row	Stitch Pattern	Done
Row 1	K30, p30, k30	
Row 2	P30, k30, p30	
Row 3	K30, p30, k30	
Row 4	P30, k30, p30	
Row 5	K30, p30, k30	
Row 6	P30, k30, p30	
Row 7	K30, p30, k30	
Row 8	P30, k30, p30	

Middle Three Letters

Row 1 K5, *customize* 20, k5, p5, *customize* 20, p5, k5, *customize* 20, k5

Row 2 P5, *customize* 20, p5, k5, *customize* 20, k5, p5, *customize* 20, p5

Row 3 K5, *customize* 20, k5, p5, *customize* 20, p5, k5, *customize* 20, k5

Row 4 P5, *customize* 20, p5, k5, *customize* 20, k5, p5, *customize* 20, p5

Row 5 K5, *customize* 20, k5, p5, *customize* 20, p5, k5, *customize* 20, k5

Row 6 P5, *customize* 20, p5, k5, *customize* 20, k5, p5, *customize* 20, p5

Row 7 K5, *customize* 20, k5, p5, *customize* 20, p5, k5, *customize* 20, k5

Row 8 P5, *customize* 20, p5, k5, *customize* 20, k5, p5, *customize* 20, p5

Row 9 K5, *customize* 20, k5, p5,

Row 10 P5, *customize* 20, p5, k5, *customize* 20, k5, p5, *customize* 20, p5

Row 11 K5, *customize* 20, k5, p5, *customize* 20, p5, k5, *customize* 20, k5

Row 12 P5, *customize* 20, p5, k5, *customize* 20, k5, p5, *customize* 20, p5

Row 13 K5, *customize* 20, k5, p5, *customize* 20, p5, k5, *customize* 20, k5

Row 14 P5, *customize* 20, p5, k5, *customize* 20, k5, p5, *customize* 20, p5

Row 15 K5, *customize* 20, k5, p5, *customize* 20, p5, k5, *ustomize* 20, k5

Row 16 P5, *customize* 20, p5, k5, *customize* 20, k5, p5, *customize* 20, p5

Row 17 K5, *customize* 20, k5, p5, *customize* 20, p5, k5, *customize* 20, k5

Row 18 P5, *customize* 20, p5, k5, *customize* 20, k5, p5, *customize* 20, p5

Row 19 K5, *customize* 20, k5, p5, *customize* 20, p5, k5, *customize* 20, k5

Row 20 P5, *customize* 20, p5, k5, *customize* 20, k5, p5, *customize* 20, p5

Row 21 K5, *customize* 20, k5, p5, *customize* 20, p5, k5, *customize* 20, k5

Starting from the top right, preceding Row 10:

customize 20, p5, k5, *customize* 20, k5

Row	Stitch Pattern	Done
Row 22	P5, *customize* 20, p5, k5, *customize* 20, k5, p5, *customize* 20, p5	
Row 23	K5, *customize* 20, k5, p5, *customize* 20, p5, k5, *customize* 20, k5	
Row 24	P5, *customize* 20, p5, k5, *customize* 20, k5, p5, *customize* 20, p5	
Row 25	K5, *customize* 20, k5, p5, *customize* 20, p5, k5, *customize* 20, k5	
Row 26	P5, *customize* 20, p5, k5, *customize* 20, k5, p5, *customize* 20, p5	
Row 27	K5, *customize* 20, k5, p5, *customize* 20, p5, k5, *customize* 20, k5	
Row 28	P5, *customize* 20, p5, k5, *customize* 20, k5, p5, *customize* 20, p5	

Upper Transition

Row	Stitch Pattern	Done
Row 1	P30, k30, p30	
Row 2	K30, p30, k30	
Row 3	P30, k30, p30	
Row 4	K30, p30, k30	
Row 5	P30, k30, p30	
Row 6	K30, p30, k30	
Row 7	P30, k30, p30	
Row 8	K30, p30, k30	

Top Three Letters

Row	Stitch Pattern	Done
Row 1	K5, *customize* 20, k5, p5, *customize* 20, p5, k5, *customize* 20, k5	
Row 2	P5, *customize* 20, p5, k5, *customize* 20, k5, p5, *customize* 20, p5	
Row 3	K5, *customize* 20, k5, p5, *customize* 20, p5, k5, *customize* 20, k5	
Row 4	P5, *customize* 20, p5, k5, *customize* 20, k5, p5, *customize* 20, p5	
Row 5	K5, *customize* 20, k5, p5, *customize* 20, p5, k5, *customize* 20, k5	
Row 6	P5, *customize* 20, p5, k5, *customize* 20, k5, p5, *customize* 20, p5	
Row 7	K5, *customize* 20, k5, p5, *customize* 20, p5, k5, *customize* 20, k5	
Row 8	P5, *customize* 20, p5, k5, *customize* 20, k5, p5, *customize* 20, p5	
Row 9	K5, *customize* 20, k5, p5, *customize* 20, p5, k5, *customize* 20, k5	
Row 10	P5, *customize* 20, p5, k5, *customize* 20, k5, p5, *customize* 20, p5	
Row 11	K5, *customize* 20, k5, p5, *customize* 20, p5, k5, *customize* 20, k5	
Row 12	P5, *customize* 20, p5, k5, *customize* 20, k5, p5, *customize* 20, p5	

Row	Stitch Pattern	Done	Row	Stitch Pattern	Done
Row 13	K5, *customize* 20, k5, p5, *customize* 20, p5, k5, *customize* 20, k5		Row 25	K5, *customize* 20, k5, p5, *customize* 20, p5, k5, *customize* 20, k5	
Row 14	P5, *customize* 20, p5, k5, *customize* 20, k5, p5, *customize* 20, p5		Row 26	P5, *customize* 20, p5, k5, *customize* 20, k5, p5, *customize* 20, p5	
Row 15	K5, *customize* 20, k5, p5, *customize* 20, p5, k5, *customize* 20, k5		Row 27	K5, *customize* 20, k5, p5, *customize* 20, p5, k5, *customize* 20, k5	
Row 16	P5, *customize* 20, p5, k5, *customize* 20, k5, p5, *customize* 20, p5		Row 28	P5, *customize* 20, p5, k5, *customize* 20, k5, p5, *customize* 20, p5	
Row 17	K5, *customize* 20, k5, p5, *customize* 20, p5, k5, *customize* 20, k5				
Row 18	P5, *customize* 20, p5, k5, *customize* 20, k5, p5, *customize* 20, p5				
Row 19	K5, *customize* 20, k5, p5, *customize* 20, p5, k5, *customize* 20, k5				
Row 20	P5, *customize* 20, p5, k5, *customize* 20, k5, p5, *customize* 20, p5				
Row 21	K5, *customize* 20, k5, p5, *customize* 20, p5, k5, *customize* 20, k5				
Row 22	P5, *customize* 20, p5, k5, *customize* 20, k5, p5, *customize* 20, p5				
Row 23	K5, *customize* 20, k5, p5, *customize* 20, p5, k5, *customize* 20, k5				
Row 24	P5, *customize* 20, p5, k5, *customize* 20, k5, p5, *customize* 20, p5				

Outside Border

Row	Stitch Pattern	Done
Row 1	K30, p30, k30	
Row 2	P30, k30, p30	
Row 3	K30, p30, k30	
Row 4	P30, k30, p30	
Row 5	K30, p30, k30	
Row 6	P30, k30, p30	
Row 7	K30, p30, k30	
Row 8	P30, k30, p30	

Cast off 90 stitches and secure loose threads.

Image on page 73.

Notes

Accessory Patterns

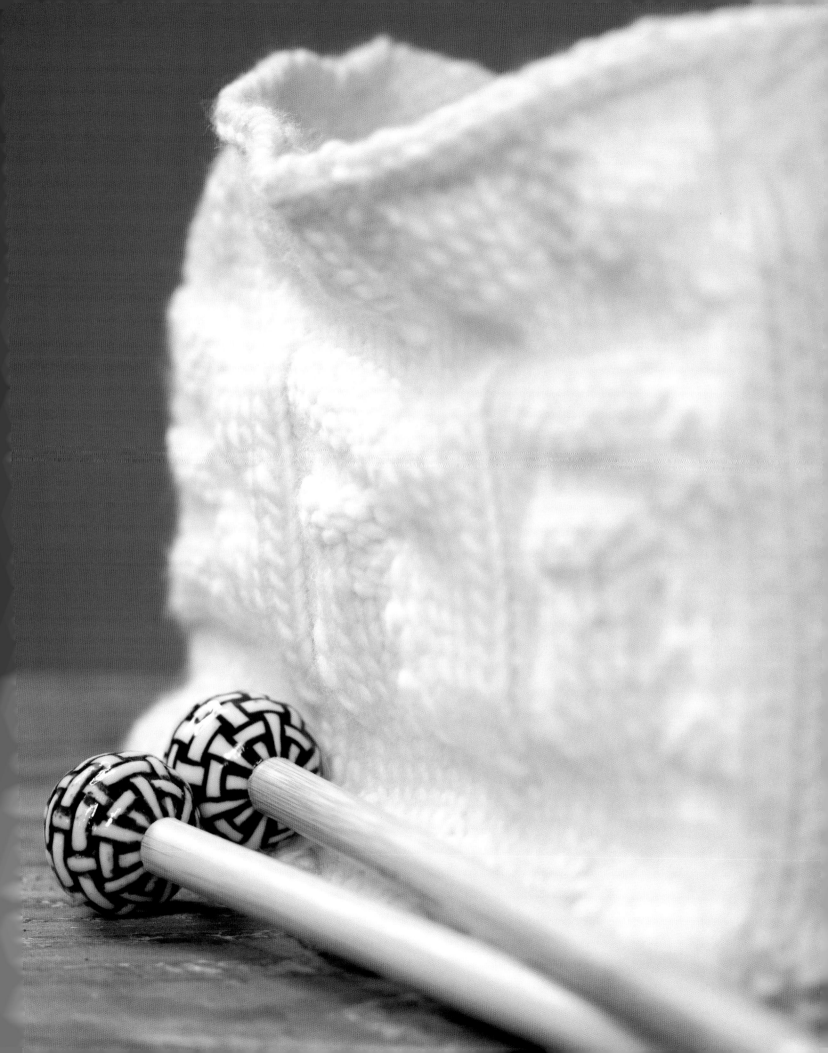

NAME SCARF

Single-Point
Needles

Yarn: Louisa Harding Grace,
50% merino wool/50% silk, 110 yds per 50g

Yards Required: 300, but this will vary greatly depending upon the
length of the name selected. Buy more yarn than you think you'll need,
just in case.

Needles: US 6 (4mm) recommended, but I used US 5 (3.75mm)

Gauge: 22 stitches and 30 rows equal 4 inches

Finished Size: Varies by number of letters in the name

Abbreviations: K (k): Knit; P (p): Purl

Cast on 40 stitches on a single-point needle.

Row	Stitch Pattern	Done	Row	Stitch Pattern	Done
Outside Border			Row 14	(P1, k1) 20 times	
			Row 15	(K1, p1) 20 times	
Row 1	K40	✓	Row 16	(P1, k1) 20 times	
Row 2	P40		Row 17	(K1, p1) 20 times	
Row 3	K40		Row 18	(P1, k1) 20 times	
Row 4	P40		Row 19	(K1, p1) 20 times	
Row 5	(K1, p1) 20 times		Row 20	(P1, k1) 20 times	
Row 6	(P1, k1) 20 times		Row 21	(K1, p1) 20 times	
Row 7	(K1, p1) 20 times		Row 22	(P1, k1) 20 times	
Row 8	(P1, k1) 20 times		Row 23	(K1, p1) 20 times	
Row 9	(K1, p1) 20 times		Row 24	P40	
Row 10	(P1, k1) 20 times		Row 25	K40	
Row 11	(K1, p1) 20 times		Row 26	P40	
Row 12	(P1, k1) 20 times		Row 27	K40	
Row 13	(K1, p1) 20 times		Row 28	P40	

Letters

Begin each row with 10 stitches of the border and end with 10 stitches of the border to reach the desired 40 stitches. "Customize 20" refers to the letter you're knitting. The first letter is the last letter of the name you're doing and letters are knit bottom to top.

Inside Border

Row	Stitch Pattern
Row 1	K40
Row 2	P40
Row 3	K40
Row 4	P40
Row 5	K40
Row 6	P40

1st Letter " ___ "

Row	Stitch Pattern
Row 1	K10, *customize* 20, k10
Row 2	P10, *customize* 20, p10
Row 3	K10, *customize* 20, k10
Row 4	P10, *customize* 20, p10
Row 5	K10, *customize* 20, k10
Row 6	P10, *customize* 20, p10
Row 7	K10, *customize* 20, k10
Row 8	P10, *customize* 20, p10
Row 9	K10, *customize* 20, k10
Row 10	P10, *customize* 20, p10
Row 11	K10, *customize* 20, k10
Row 12	P10, *customize* 20, p10
Row 13	K10, *customize* 20, k10
Row 14	P10, *customize* 20, p10
Row 15	K10, *customize* 20, k10
Row 16	P10, *customize* 20, p10
Row 17	K10, *customize* 20, k10
Row 18	P10, *customize* 20, p10
Row 19	K10, *customize* 20, k10
Row 20	P10, *customize* 20, p10
Row 21	K10, *customize* 20, k10
Row 22	P10, *customize* 20, p10
Row 23	K10, *customize* 20, k10
Row 24	P10, *customize* 20, p10
Row 25	K10, *customize* 20, k10
Row 26	P10, *customize* 20, p10
Row 27	K10, *customize* 20, k10
Row 28	P10, customize 20, p10

Second Letter " ___ "

Row	Stitch Pattern
Row 1	K10, *customize* 20, k10
Row 2	P10, *customize* 20, p10
Row 3	K10, *customize* 20, k10
Row 4	P10, *customize* 20, p10
Row 5	K10, *customize* 20, k10
Row 6	P10, *customize* 20, p10
Row 7	K10, *customize* 20, k10
Row 8	P10, *customize* 20, p10
Row 9	K10, *customize* 20, k10
Row 10	P10, *customize* 20, p10
Row 11	K10, *customize* 20, k10
Row 12	P10, *customize* 20, p10
Row 13	K10, *customize* 20, k10
Row 14	P10, *customize* 20, p10
Row 15	K10, *customize* 20, k10
Row 16	P10, *customize* 20, p10
Row 17	K10, *customize* 20, k10
Row 18	P10, *customize* 20, p10
Row 19	K10, *customize* 20, k10
Row 20	P10, *customize* 20, p10
Row 21	K10, *customize* 20, k10
Row 22	P10, *customize* 20, p10
Row 23	K10, *customize* 20, k10
Row 24	P10, *customize* 20, p10
Row 25	K10, *customize* 20, k10
Row 26	P10, *customize* 20, p10
Row 27	K10, *customize* 20, k10
Row 28	P10, *customize* 20, p10

Inside Border

Row 26	P10, *customize* 20, p10

Row 1   K40
Row 2   P40
Row 3   K40
Row 4   P40
Row 5   K40
Row 6   P40

Row 26   P10, *customize* 20, p10
Row 27   K10, *customize* 20, k10
Row 28   P10, *customize* 20, p10

Inside Border

Row 1   K40
Row 2   P40
Row 3   K40
Row 4   P40
Row 5   K40
Row 6   P40

Third Letter "＿＿＿"

Row 1   K10, *customize* 20, k10
Row 2   P10, *customize* 20, p10
Row 3   K10, *customize* 20, k10
Row 4   P10, *customize* 20, p10
Row 5   K10, *customize* 20, k10
Row 6   P10, *customize* 20, p10
Row 7   K10, *customize* 20, k10
Row 8   P10, *customize* 20, p10
Row 9   K10, *customize* 20, k10
Row 10   P10, *customize* 20, p10
Row 11   K10, *customize* 20, k10
Row 12   P10, *customize* 20, p10
Row 13   K10, *customize* 20, k10
Row 14   P10, *customize* 20, p10
Row 15   K10, *customize* 20, k10
Row 16   P10, *customize* 20, p10
Row 17   K10, *customize* 20, k10
Row 18   P10, *customize* 20, p10
Row 19   K10, *customize* 20, k10
Row 20   P10, *customize* 20, p10
Row 21   K10, *customize* 20, k10
Row 22   P10, *customize* 20, p10
Row 23   K10, *customize* 20, k10
Row 24   P10, *customize* 20, p10
Row 25   K10, *customize* 20, k10

Fourth Letter "＿＿＿"

Row 1   K10, *customize* 20, k10
Row 2   P10, *customize* 20, p10
Row 2   K10, *customize* 20, k10
Row 4   P10, *customize* 20, p10
Row 5   K10, *customize* 20, k10
Row 6   P10, *customize* 20, p10
Row 7   K10, *customize* 20, k10
Row 8   P10, *customize* 20, p10
Row 9   K10, *customize* 20, k10
Row 10   P10, *customize* 20, p10
Row 11   K10, *customize* 20, k10
Row 12   P10, *customize* 20, p10
Row 13   K10, *customize* 20, k10
Row 14   P10, *customize* 20, p10
Row 15   K10, *customize* 20, k10
Row 16   P10, *customize* 20, p10
Row 17   K10, *customize* 20, k10
Row 18   P10, *customize* 20, p10
Row 19   K10, *customize* 20, k10
Row 20   P10, *customize* 20, p10

Row	Stitch Pattern	Done
Row 21	K10, *customize* 20, k10	
Row 22	P10, *customize* 20, p10	
Row 23	K10, *customize* 20, k10	
Row 24	P10, *customize* 20, p10	
Row 25	K10, *customize* 20, k10	
Row 26	P10, *customize* 20, p10	
Row 27	K10, *customize* 20, k10	
Row 28	P10, *customize* 20, p10	

Inside Border

Row	Stitch Pattern	Done
Row 1	K40	
Row 2	P40	
Row 3	K40	
Row 4	P40	
Row 5	K40	
Row 6	P40	

Fifth Letter "____"

Row	Stitch Pattern	Done
Row 1	K10, *customize* 20, k10	
Row 2	P10, *customize* 20, p10	
Row 3	K10, *customize* 20, k10	
Row 4	P10, *customize* 20, p10	
Row 5	K10, *customize* 20, k10	
Row 6	P10, *customize* 20, p10	
Row 7	K10, *customize* 20, k10	
Row 8	P10, *customize* 20, p10	
Row 9	K10, *customize* 20, k10	
Row 10	P10, *customize* 20, p10	
Row 11	K10, *customize* 20, k10	
Row 12	P10, *customize* 20, p10	
Row 13	K10, *customize* 20, k10	
Row 14	P10, *customize* 20, p10	
Row 15	K10, *customize* 20, k10	

Row	Stitch Pattern	Done
Row 16	P10, *customize* 20, p10	
Row 17	K10, *customize* 20, k10	
Row 18	P10, *customize* 20, p10	
Row 19	K10, *customize* 20, k10	
Row 20	P10, *customize* 20, p10	
Row 21	K10, *customize* 20, k10	
Row 22	P10, *customize* 20, p10	
Row 23	K10, *customize* 20, k10	
Row 24	P10, *customize* 20, p10	
Row 25	K10, *customize* 20, k10	
Row 26	P10, *customize* 20, p10	
Row 27	K10, *customize* 20, k10	
Row 28	P10, *customize* 20, p10	

Inside Border

Row	Stitch Pattern	Done
Row 1	K40	
Row 2	P40	
Row 3	K40	
Row 4	P40	
Row 5	K40	
Row 6	P40	

Sixth Letter "____"

Row	Stitch Pattern	Done
Row 1	K10, *customize* 20, k10	
Row 2	P10, *customize* 20, p10	
Row 3	K10, *customize* 20, k10	
Row 4	P10, *customize* 20, p10	
Row 5	K10, *customize* 20, k10	
Row 6	P10, *customize* 20, p10	
Row 7	K10, *customize* 20, k10	
Row 8	P10, *customize* 20, p10	
Row 9	K10, *customize* 20, k10	
Row 10	P10, *customize* 20, p10	

Row 11	K10, *customize* 20, k10		Row 8	P10, *customize* 20, p10	
Row 12	P10, *customize* 20, p10		Row 9	K10, *customize* 20, k10	
Row 13	K10, *customize* 20, k10		Row 10	P10, *customize* 20, p10	
Row 14	P10, *customize* 20, p10		Row 11	K10, *customize* 20, k10	
Row 15	K10, *customize* 20, k10		Row 12	P10, *customize* 20, p10	
Row 16	P10, *customize* 20, p10		Row 13	K10, *customize* 20, k10	
Row 17	K10, *customize* 20, k10		Row 14	P10, *customize* 20, p10	
Row 18	P10, *customize* 20, p10		Row 15	K10, *customize* 20, k10	
Row 19	K10, *customize* 20, k10		Row 16	P10, *customize* 20, p10	
Row 20	P10, *customize* 20, p10		Row 17	K10, *customize* 20, k10	
Row 21	K10, *customize* 20, k10		Row 18	P10, *customize* 20, p10	
Row 22	P10, *customize* 20, p10		Row 19	K10, *customize* 20, k10	
Row 23	K10, *customize* 20, k10		Row 20	P10, *customize* 20, p10	
Row 24	P10, *customize* 20, p10		Row 21	K10, *customize* 20, k10	
Row 25	K10, *customize* 20, k10		Row 22	P10, *customize* 20, p10	
Row 26	P10, *customize* 20, p10		Row 23	K10, *customize* 20, k10	
Row 27	K10, *customize* 20, k10		Row 24	P10, *customize* 20, p10	
Row 28	P10, *customize* 20, p10		Row 25	K10, *customize* 20, k10	
			Row 26	P10, *customize* 20, p10	
			Row 27	K10, *customize* 20, k10	
			Row 28	P10, *customize* 20, p10	

Inside Border

Row 1	K40
Row 2	P40
Row 3	K40
Row 4	P40
Row 5	K40
Row 6	P40

Inside Border

Row 1	K40
Row 2	P40
Row 3	K40
Row 4	P40
Row 5	K40
Row 6	P40

Seventh Letter "____"

Row 1	K10, *customize* 20, k10
Row 2	P10, *customize* 20, p10
Row 3	K10, *customize* 20, k10
Row 4	P10, *customize* 20, p10
Row 5	K10, *customize* 20, k10
Row 6	P10, *customize* 20, p10
Row 7	K10, *customize* 20, k10

Eighth Letter "____"

Row 1	K10, *customize* 20, k10
Row 2	P10, *customize* 20, p10
Row 3	K10, *customize* 20, k10
Row 4	P10, *customize* 20, p10

Row	Stitch Pattern	Done
Row 5	K10, *customize* 20, k10	
Row 6	P10, *customize* 20, p10	
Row 7	K10, *customize* 20, k10	
Row 8	P10, *customize* 20, p10	
Row 9	K10, *customize* 20, k10	
Row 10	P10, *customize* 20, p10	
Row 11	K10, *customize* 20, k10	
Row 12	P10, *customize* 20, p10	
Row 13	K10, *customize* 20, k10	
Row 14	P10, *customize* 20, p10	
Row 15	K10, *customize* 20, k10	
Row 16	P10, *customize* 20, p10	
Row 17	K10, *customize* 20, k10	
Row 18	P10, *customize* 20, p10	
Row 19	K10, *customize* 20, k10	
Row 20	P10, *customize* 20, p10	
Row 21	K10, *customize* 20, k10	
Row 22	P10, *customize* 20, p10	
Row 23	K10, *customize* 20, k10	
Row 24	P10, *customize* 20, p10	
Row 25	K10, *customize* 20, k10	
Row 26	P10, *customize* 20, p10	
Row 27	K10, *customize* 20, k10	
Row 28	P10, *customize* 20, p10	

Templates for eight custom letters have been provided but please continue in the same manner until the full name and/or desired length has been achieved. After the last letter, end your project with the Outside Border.

Outside Border

Row	Stitch Pattern	Done
Row 1	K40	
Row 2	P40	
Row 3	K40	
Row 4	P40	
Row 5	(K1, p1) 20 times	
Row 6	(P1, k1) 20 times	
Row 7	(K1, p1) 20 times	
Row 8	P1, k1) 20 times	
Row 9	(K1, p1) 20 times	
Row 10	P1, k1) 20 times	
Row 11	(K1, p1) 20 times	
Row 12	P1, k1) 20 times	
Row 13	(K1, p1) 20 times	
Row 14	P1, k1) 20 times	
Row 15	(K1, p1) 20 times	
Row 16	P1, k1) 20 times	
Row 17	(K1, p1) 20 times	
Row 18	P1, k1) 20 times	
Row 19	(K1, p1) 20 times	
Row 20	P1, k1) 20 times	
Row 21	(K1, p1) 20 times	
Row 22	P1, k1) 20 times	
Row 23	(K1, p1) 20 times	
Row 24	P40	
Row 25	K40	
Row 26	P40	
Row 27	K40	
Row 28	P40	

Cast off 40 stitches and secure loose threads.

SIGNATURE INITIAL SCARF

Single-Point
Needles

Yarn: Berroco Ultra Alpaca,
50% alpaca/50% wool,
215 yd per 100g

Yards Required: 300 but this will vary greatly depending upon the
length of the name selected. Buy more yarn than you think you'll need, just in case.

Needles: US 8 (5mm)

Gauge: 20 stitches and 26 rows equal 4 inches

Finished Size: Varies by number of repeat showings of the initials

Abbreviations: K (k): Knit; P (p): Purl

Cast on 48 stitches on a single-point needle.

Row	Stitch Pattern	Done

Outside Border

Row 1	K48	✓
Row 2	K48	
Row 3	P48	
Row 4	P48	
Row 5	K48	
Row 6	K48	
Row 7	P48	
Row 8	P48	
Row 9	K48	
Row 10	K48	
Row 11	P48	
Row 12	P48	
Row 13	K48	

Row	Stitch Pattern	Done
Row 14	K48	
Row 15	P48	
Row 16	P48	

Below the Letter

Row 1	K48	
Row 2	K8, p32, k8	
Row 3	P8, k32, p8	
Row 4	P48	
Row 5	K48	
Row 6	K8, p32, k8	
Row 7	P8, k32, p8	
Row 8	P48	

Letters

Begin each row with 14 stitches of the border and end with 14 stitches of the border to reach the desired 48 stitches. "Customize 20" refers to the letter you're knitting. The first letter is the last letter of the name you are doing and letters are knit bottom to top.

First Letter "_____"

Row	Stitch Pattern
Row 1	K14, *customize* 20, k14
Row 2	K8, p6, *customize* 20, p6, k8
Row 3	P8, k6, *customize* 20, k6, p8
Row 4	P14, *customize* 20, p14
Row 5	K14, *customize* 20, k14
Row 6	K8, p6, *customize* 20, p6, k8
Row 7	P8, k6, *customize* 20, k6, p8
Row 8	P14, *customize* 20, p14
Row 9	K14, *customize* 20, k14
Row 10	K8, p6, *customize* 20, p6, k8
Row 11	P8, k6, *customize* 20, k6, p8
Row 12	P14, *customize* 20, p14
Row 13	K14, *customize* 20, k14
Row 14	K8, p6, *customize* 20, p6, k8
Row 15	P8, k6, *customize* 20, k6, p8
Row 16	P14, *customize* 20, p14
Row 17	K14, *customize* 20, k14
Row 18	K8, p6, *customize* 20, p6, k8
Row 19	P8, k6, *customize* 20, k6, p8
Row 20	P14, *customize* 20, p14
Row 21	K14, *customize* 20, k14
Row 22	K8, p6, *customize* 20, p6, k8
Row 23	P8, k6, *customize* 20, k6, p8
Row 24	P14, *customize* 20, p14
Row 25	K14, *customize* 20, k14
Row 26	K8, p6, *customize* 20, p6, k8
Row 27	P8, k6, *customize* 20, k6, p8
Row 28	P14, *customize* 20, p14

Above the Letter

Row	Stitch Pattern
Row 1	K48
Row 2	K8, p32, k8
Row 3	P8, k32, p8
Row 4	P48
Row 5	K48
Row 6	K8, p32, k8
Row 7	P8, k32, p8
Row 8	P48

Inside Border

Row	Stitch Pattern
Row 1	K48
Row 2	K48
Row 3	P48
Row 4	P48
Row 5	K48
Row 6	K48
Row 7	P48
Row 8	P48

Below the Letter

Row	Stitch Pattern
Row 1	K48
Row 2	K8, p32, k8
Row 3	P8, k32, p8
Row 4	P48
Row 5	K48
Row 6	K8, p32, k8
Row 7	P8, k32, p8
Row 8	P48

Second Letter "＿＿"

Row	Stitch Pattern
Row 1	K14, *customize* 20, k14
Row 2	K8, p6, *customize* 20, p6, k8
Row 3	P8, k6, *customize* 20, k6, p8
Row 4	P14, *customize* 20, p14
Row 5	K14, *customize* 20, k14
Row 6	K8, p6, *customize* 20, p6, k8
Row 7	P8, k6, *customize* 20, k6, p8
Row 8	P14, *customize* 20, p14
Row 9	K14, *customize* 20, k14
Row 10	K8, p6, *customize* 20, p6, k8
Row 11	P8, k6, *customize* 20, k6, p8
Row 12	P14, *customize* 20, p14
Row 13	K14, *customize* 20, k14
Row 14	K8, p6, *customize* 20, p6, k8
Row 15	P8, k6, *customize* 20, k6, p8
Row 16	P14, *customize* 20, p14
Row 17	K14, *customize* 20, k14
Row 18	K8, p6, *customize* 20, p6, k8
Row 19	P8, k6, *customize* 20, k6, p8
Row 20	P14, *customize* 20, p14
Row 21	K14, *customize* 20, k14
Row 22	K8, p6, *customize* 20, p6, k8
Row 23	P8, k6, *customize* 20, k6, p8
Row 24	P14, *customize* 20, p14
Row 25	K14, *customize* 20, k14
Row 26	K8, p6, *customize* 20, p6, k8
Row 27	P8, k6, *customize* 20, k6, p8
Row 28	P14, *customize* 20, p14

Above the Letter

Row	Stitch Pattern
Row 1	K48
Row 2	K8, p32, k8
Row 3	P8, k32, p8
Row 4	P48
Row 5	K48

Row	Stitch Pattern
Row 6	K8, p32, k8
Row 7	P8, k32, p8
Row 8	P48

Inside Border

Row	Stitch Pattern
Row 1	K48
Row 2	K48
Row 3	P48
Row 4	P48
Row 5	K48
Row 6	K48
Row 7	P48
Row 8	P48

Below the Letter

Row	Stitch Pattern
Row 1	K48
Row 2	K8, p32, k8
Row 3	P8, k32, p8
Row 4	P48
Row 5	K48
Row 6	K8, p32, k8
Row 7	P8, k32, p8
Row 8	P48

Third Letter "＿＿"

Row	Stitch Pattern
Row 1	K14, *customize* 20, k14
Row 2	K8, p6, *customize* 20, p6, k8
Row 3	P8, k6, *customize* 20, k6, p8
Row 4	P14, *customize* 20, p14
Row 5	K14, *customize* 20, k14
Row 6	K8, p6, *customize* 20, p6, k8
Row 7	P8, k6, *customize* 20, k6, p8
Row 8	P14, *customize* 20, p14

Row · · · · · · Stitch Pattern · · · · · · · · · · · · · · Done

Row 9   K14, *customize* 20, k14
Row 10   K8, p6, *customize* 20, p6, k8
Row 11   P8, k6, *customize* 20, k6, p8
Row 12   P14, *customize* 20, p14
Row 13   K14, *customize* 20, k14
Row 14   K8, p6, *customize* 20, p6, k8
Row 15   P8, k6, *customize* 20, k6, p8
Row 16   P14, *customize* 20, p14
Row 17   K14, *customize* 20, k14
Row 18   K8, p6, *customize* 20, p6, k8
Row 19   P8, k6, *customize* 20, k6, p8
Row 20   P14, *customize* 20, p14
Row 21   K14, *customize* 20, k14
Row 22   K8, p6, *customize* 20, p6, k8
Row 23   P8, k6, *customize* 20, k6, p8
Row 24   P14, *customize* 20, p14
Row 25   K14, *customize* 20, k14
Row 26   K8, p6, *customize* 20, p6, k8
Row 27   P8, k6, *customize* 20, k6, p8
Row 28   P14, *customize* 20, p14

Above the Letter

Row 1   K48
Row 2   K8, p32, k8
Row 3   P8, k32, p8
Row 4   P48
Row 5   K48
Row 6   K8, p32, k8
Row 7   P8, k32, p8
Row 8   P48

· ·

Most people use three letters; repeat these three letters three or four times until you reach the desired length, then finish with the Outside Border.

· ·

Row · · · · · · Stitch Pattern · · · · · · · · · · · · Done

Outside Border

Row 1   K48
Row 2   K48
Row 3   P48
Row 4   P48
Row 5   K48
Row 6   K48
Row 7   P48
Row 8   P48
Row 9   K48
Row 10   K48
Row 11   P48
Row 12   P48
Row 13   K48
Row 14   K48
Row 15   P48
Row 16   P48

· ·

Cast off 48 stitches and secure loose threads.

· ·

SINGLE INITIAL MITTEN

Single-Point
Needles

Yarn: Berroco Ultra Alpaca,
50% alpaca/50% wool, 215 yd per 100g

Yards Required: 75

Needles: US 8 (5mm) recommended, but I used US 5 (3.75mm)

Gauge: 20 stitches and 26 rows equal 4 inches

Finished Size: To fit most adults

Abbreviations: K (k): Knit; P (p): Purl
inc 1: Knit into the front and the back of the next stitch (one stitch increased)
k2tog: Knit 2 stitches together as 1 (one stitch decreased)

Cast on 36 stitches on a single-point needle.

Row	Stitch Pattern	Total # of Stitches	Done	Row	Stitch Pattern	Total # of Stitches	Done
Cuff Section				Row 14	(K1, p1) 18 times	36	
				Row 15	(K1, p1) 18 times	36	
Row 1	(K1, p1) 18 times	36	✓	Row 16	(K1, p1) 18 times	36	
Row 2	(K1, p1) 18 times	36		Row 17	(K1, p1) 18 times	36	
Row 3	(K1, p1) 18 times	36		Row 18	(K1, p1) 18 times	36	
Row 4	(K1, p1) 18 times	36		Row 19	(K1, p1) 18 times	36	
Row 5	(K1, p1) 18 times	36		Row 20	(K1, p1) 18 times	36	
Row 6	(K1, p1) 18 times	36		Row 21	(K1, p1) 18 times	36	
Row 7	(K1, p1) 18 times	36		Row 22	(K1, p1) 18 times	36	
Row 8	(K1, p1) 18 times	36		Row 23	(K1, p1) 18 times	36	
Row 9	(K1, p1) 18 times	36		Row 24	(K1, p1) 18 times	36	
Row 10	(K1, p1) 18 times	36		Row 25	(K1, p1) 18 times	36	
Row 11	(K1, p1) 18 times	36		Row 26	(K1, p1) 18 times	36	
Row 12	(K1, p1) 18 times	36		Row 27	(K1, p1) 18 times	36	
Row 13	(K1, p1) 18 times	36		Row 28	(K1, p1) 18 times	36	

Hand

Row	Stitch Pattern	Total # of Stitches	Done
Row 1	K1, inc 1, k32, inc 1, k1	38	
Row 2	P38	38	
Row 3	K38	38	
Row 4	P38	38	
Row 5	K38	38	
Row 6	P38	38	
Row 7	K38	38	
Row 8	P38	38	
Row 9	K38	38	
Row 10	P38	38	
Row 11	K2, inc 1, k32, inc 1, k2	40	
Row 12	P40	40	
Row 13	K19, inc 1 two times, k19	42	
Row 14	P42	42	
Row 15	K19, inc 1, k2, inc 1, k19	44	
Row 16	P44	44	
Row 17	K19, inc 1, k4, inc 1, k19	46	
Row 18	P46	46	
Row 19	K19, inc 1, k6, inc 1, k19	48	
Row 20	P48	48	
Row 21	K19, inc 1, k8, inc 1, k19	50	
Row 22	P50	50	
Row 23	K19, inc 1, k10, inc 1, k19	52	
Row 24	P52	52	
Row 25	K19, move 14 to holder, k19	38	
Row 26	P38	38	
Row 27	K38	38	
Row 28	P38	38	
Row 29	K38	38	
Row 30	P38	38	

Right Mitten

Row	Stitch Pattern	Total # of Stitches	Done
Row 1	K5, *customize* 10, k23		
Row 2	P23, *customize* 10, p5		
Row 3	K5, *customize* 10, k23		
Row 4	P23, *customize* 10, p5		
Row 5	K5, *customize* 10, k23		
Row 7	K5, *customize* 10, k23		
Row 8	P23, *customize* 10, p5		
Row 9	K5, *customize* 10, k23		
Row 10	P23, *customize* 10, p5		
Row 11	K5, *customize* 10, k23		
Row 12	P23, *customize* 10, p5		
Row 13	K5, *customize* 10, k23		
Row 14	P23, *customize* 10, p5		

Left Mitten

Row	Stitch Pattern	Total # of Stitches	Done
Row 1	K23, *customize* 10, k5		
Row 2	P5, *customize* 10, p23		
Row 3	K23, *customize* 10, k5		
Row 4	P5, *customize* 10, p23		
Row 5	K23, *customize* 10, k5		
Row 7	K23, *customize* 10, k5		
Row 8	P5, *customize* 10, p23		
Row 9	K23, *customize* 10, k5		
Row 10	P5, *customize* 10, p23		
Row 11	K23, *customize* 10, k5		
Row 12	P5, *customize* 10, p23		
Row 13	K23, *customize* 10, k5		
Row 14	P5, *customize* 10, p23		

Hands

Row	Stitch Pattern	Total # of Stitches
Row 1	K38	
Row 2	P38	38
Row 3	(K2, k2tog) 9 times, k2	29
Row 4	P29	29
Row 5	(K1, k2tog) 9 times, k2	20
Row 6	P20	20
Row 7	K2tog 10 times	10

Cut the yarn leaving a long tail of yarn. Thread the tail onto a darning needle pass through the remaining 10 stitches. Pull gently. Secure yarn on back side.

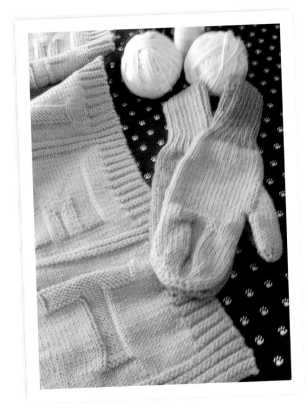

Thumb

Transfer stitches from needle holder back on to single-point needle with purl stitches facing you.

Row	Stitch Pattern	Total # of Stitches
Row 1	P14	14
Row 2	K14	14
Row 3	P14	14
Row 4	K14	14
Row 5	P14	14
Row 6	K14	14
Row 7	P14	14
Row 8	K14	14
Row 9	P14	14
Row 10	K14	14
Row 11	P14	14
Row 12	K2tog 7 times	7

Cut the yarn leaving a long tail. Thread the tail onto a darning needle and pass through the remaining 10 stitches. Pull gently. Secure yarn on back side. Fold the mitten in half with knit sides facing one another. Stitch mitten together. Turn outside-in.

INITIAL GLOVE-ETTE

Single-Point Needles

Yarn: jill eaton Minnow Merino,
100% extra fine superwash merino wool,
77 yds per 50g

Yards Required: 100

Needles: US 8 (5mm)

Gauge: 18 stitches equal 4 inches

Finished Size: To fit most adults

Abbreviations: K (k): Knit; P (p): Purl

Cast on 44 stitches on a single-point needle.

A left and right version make the perfect pair. Each glove-ette has 22 rows with a letter for the front and 22 plain rows for the back. Note that this initial is knit east/west as opposed to north/south, so you'll need to adjust the normal grid layouts to suit your favorite letter.

Row	Stitch Pattern	Done
Left Hand Front		
Row 1	K32, p1, k1, p1, k1, k4, p1, k1, p1, k1	✓
Row 2	K1, p1, k1, p1, p4, k1, p1, k1, p1, p32	
Row 3	K32, p1, k1, p1, k1, k4, p1, k1, p1, k1	
Row 4	K1, p1, k1, p1, p4, k1, p1, k1, p1, p32	
Row 5	K32, p1, k1, p1, k1, k4, p1, k1, p1, k1	
Letter		
Row 1	K1, p1, k1, p1, p4, k1, p1, k1, p1, p16, *customize* 14, p2	
Row 2	K2, *customize* 14, k16, p1, k1, p1, k1, k4, p1, k1, p1, k1	

Row	Stitch Pattern	Done
Row 3	K1, p1, k1, p1, p4, k1, p1, k1, p1, p16, *customize* 14, p2	
Row 4	K2, *customize* 14, k16, p1, k1, p1, k1, k4, p1, k1, p1, k1	
Row 5	K1, p1, k1, p1, p4, k1, p1, k1, p1, p16, *customize* 14, p2	
Row 6	K2, customize 14, k16, p1, k1, p1, k1, k4, p1, k1, p1, k1	
Row 7	K1, p1, k1, p1, p4, k1, p1, k1, p1, p16, *customize* 14, p2	
Row 8	K2, *customize* 14, k16, p1, k1, p1, k1, k4, p1, k1, p1, k1	
Row 9	K1, p1, k1, p1, p4, k1, p1, k1, p1, p16, *customize* 14, p2	

Row	Stitch Pattern	Done
Row 10	K2, customize 14, k16, p1, k1, p1, k1, k4, p1, k1, p1, k1	
Row 11	K1, p1, k1, p1, p4, k1, p1, k1, p1, p16, *customize* 14, p2	
Row 12	K2, customize 14, k16, p1, k1, p1, k1, k4, p1, k1, p1, k1	
Row 13	K1, p1, k1, p1, p4, k1, p1, k1, p1, p32	
Row 14	K32, p1, k1, p1, k1, k4, p1, k1, p1, k1	
Row 15	K1, p1, k1, p1, p4, k1, p1, k1, p1, p32	
Row 16	K32, p1, k1, p1, k1, k4, p1, k1, p1, k1	
Row 17	K1, p1, k1, p1, p4, k1, p1, k1, p1, p32	

Cast off 44 stitches and secure loose threads.

Turn piece so the letter is at the bottom. Fold the piece with right sides together. Start at the bottom and stitch closed approximately six rows. Secure the thread. Leave an opening of approximately eight rows for the thumb and then stitch closed the remainder of the piece. Secure thread. Turn back to right side. You have just completed the left hand.

Left Hand Back

Row	Stitch Pattern	Done
Row 1	K32, p1, k1, p1, k1, k4, p1, k1, p1, k1	
Row 2	K1, p1, k1, p1, p4, k1, p1, k1, p1, p32	
Row 3	K32, p1, k1, p1, k1, k4, p1, k1, p1, k1	
Row 4	K1, p1, k1, p1, p4, k1, p1, k1, p1, p32	
Row 5	K32, p1, k1, p1, k1, k4, p1, k1, p1, k1	
Row 6	K1, p1, k1, p1, p4, k1, p1, k1, p1, p32	
Row 7	K32, p1, k1, p1, k1, k4, p1, k1, p1, k1	
Row 8	K1, p1, k1, p1, p4, k1, p1, k1, p1, p32	
Row 9	K32, p1, k1, p1, k1, k4, p1, k1, p1, k1	
Row 10	K1, p1, k1, p1, p4, k1, p1, k1, p1, p32	
Row 11	K32, p1, k1, p1, k1, k4, p1, k1, p1, k1	
Row 12	K1, p1, k1, p1, p4, k1, p1, k1, p1, p32	
Row 13	K32, p1, k1, p1, k1, k4, p1, k1, p1, k1	
Row 14	K1, p1, k1, p1, p4, k1, p1, k1, p1, p32	
Row 15	K32, p1, k1, p1, k1, k4, p1, k1, p1, k1	
Row 16	K1, p1, k1, p1, p4, k1, p1, k1, p1, p32	
Row 17	K32, p1, k1, p1, k1, k4, p1, k1, p1, k1	
Row 18	K1, p1, k1, p1, p4, k1, p1, k1, p1, p32	
Row 19	K32, p1, k1, p1, k1, k4, p1, k1, p1, k1	
Row 20	K1, p1, k1, p1, p4, k1, p1, k1, p1, p32	
Row 21	K32, p1, k1, p1, k1, k4, p1, k1, p1, k1	
Row 22	K1, p1, k1, p1, p4, k1, p1, k1, p1, p32	

Right Hand Back

Row	Stitch Pattern	Done
Row 1	K32, p1, k1, p1, k1, k4, p1, k1, p1, k1	
Row 2	K1, p1, k1, p1, p4, k1, p1, k1, p1, p32	
Row 3	K32, p1, k1, p1, k1, k4, p1, k1, p1, k1	
Row 4	K1, p1, k1, p1, p4, k1, p1, k1, p1, p32	
Row 5	K32, p1, k1, p1, k1, k4, p1, k1, p1, k1	
Row 6	K1, p1, k1, p1, p4, k1, p1, k1, p1, p32	
Row 7	K32, p1, k1, p1, k1, k4, p1, k1, p1, k1	
Row 8	K1, p1, k1, p1, p4, k1, p1, k1, p1, p32	
Row 9	K32, p1, k1, p1, k1, k4, p1, k1, p1, k1	
Row 10	K1, p1, k1, p1, p4, k1, p1, k1, p1, p32	
Row 11	K32, p1, k1, p1, k1, k4, p1, k1, p1, k1	
Row 12	K1, p1, k1, p1, p4, k1, p1, k1, p1, p32	
Row 13	K32, p1, k1, p1, k1, k4, p1, k1, p1, k1	
Row 14	K1, p1, k1, p1, p4, k1, p1, k1, p1, p32	
Row 15	K32, p1, k1, p1, k1, k4, p1, k1, p1, k1	
Row 16	K1, p1, k1, p1, p4, k1, p1, k1, p1, p32	
Row 17	K32, p1, k1, p1, k1, k4, p1, k1, p1, k1	
Row 18	K1, p1, k1, p1, p4, k1, p1, k1, p1, p32	
Row 19	K32, p1, k1, p1, k1, k4, p1, k1, p1, k1	
Row 20	K1, p1, k1, p1, p4, k1, p1, k1, p1, p32	
Row 21	K32, p1, k1, p1, k1, k4, p1, k1, p1, k1	
Row 22	K1, p1, k1, p1, p4, k1, p1, k1, p1, p32	

Letter

Row	Stitch Pattern
Row 1	K1, p1, k1, p1, p4, k1, p1, k1, p1, p16, *customize* 14, p2
Row 2	K2, *customize* 14, k16, p1, k1, p1, k1, k4, p1, k1, p1, k1
Row 3	K1, p1, k1, p1, p4, k1, p1, k1, p1, p16, *customize* 14, p2
Row 4	K2, *customize* 14, k16, p1, k1, p1, k1, k4, p1, k1, p1, k1
Row 5	K1, p1, k1, p1, p4, k1, p1, k1, p1, p16, *customize* 14, p2
Row 6	K2, customize 14, k16, p1, k1, p1, k1, k4, p1, k1, p1, k1
Row 7	K1, p1, k1, p1, p4, k1, p1, k1, p1, p16, *customize* 14, p2
Row 8	K2, *customize* 14, k16, p1, k1, p1, k1, k4, p1, k1, p1, k1
Row 9	K1, p1, k1, p1, p4, k1, p1, k1, p1, p16, *customize* 14, p2
Row 10	K2, *customize* 14, k16, p1, k1, p1, k1, k4, p1, k1, p1, k1
Row 11	K1, p1, k1, p1, p4, k1, p1, k1, p1, p16, *customize* 14, p2
Row 12	K2, *customize* 14, k16, p1, k1, p1, k1, k4, p1, k1, p1, k1
Row 13	K1, p1, k1, p1, p4, k1, p1, k1, p1, p32
Row 14	K32, p1, k1, p1, k1, k4, p1, k1, p1, k1
Row 15	K1, p1, k1, p1, p4, k1, p1, k1, p1, p32
Row 16	K32, p1, k1, p1, k1, k4, p1, k1, p1, k1
Row 17	K1, p1, k1, p1, p4, k1, p1, k1, p1, p32

Right Hand Front

Row	Stitch Pattern
Row 1	K32, p1, k1, p1, k1, k4, p1, k1, p1, k1
Row 2	K1, p1, k1, p1, p4, k1, p1, k1, p1, p32
Row 3	K32, p1, k1, p1, k1, k4, p1, k1, p1, k1
Row 4	K1, p1, k1, p1, p4, k1, p1, k1, p1, p32
Row 5	K32, p1, k1, p1, k1, k4, p1, k1, p1, k1

Cast off 44 stitches and secure loose threads.

Turn piece so the letter is at the bottom. Fold the piece with right sides together. Start at the bottom and stitch closed approximately six rows. Secure the thread. Leave an opening of approximately eight rows for the thumb and then stitch closed the remainder of the piece. Secure thread. Turn back to right side. You have just completed the right hand. Now you have the perfect pair!

SIGNATURE INITIAL NECK WARMER

Circular
Needle

Yarn: Mary Jo Cole, 100% cashmere

Yards Required: 100

Needles: US 8 (5mm), 16 inch circular, 1 US 8 (5mm) single-point, 4 US 8 (5mm) double-points

Gauge: 18 stitches and 24 rows equal 4 inches

Finished Size: 18 stitches equal 4 inches

Abbreviations: K (k): Knit; P (p): Purl

Cast on 88 stitches on a straight needle and then transfer them to the circular one. Place a marker in front of first stitch to indicate beginning of the round. Join for knitting in the round.

jil eaton Minnow Merino, 100% extra fine merino wool with a gauge of 4.5 stitches to one inch is a wonderful alternative yarn for this project.

Round	Stitch Pattern	Done
Bottom Border		
Round 1	(K4, p1, k1, p1, k1) 11 times	✓
Round 2	(K4, k1, p1, k1, p1) 11 times	
Round 3	(K4, p1, k1, p1, k1) 11 times	
Round 4	(K4, k1, p1, k1, p1) 11 times	
Round 5	(K4, p1, k1, p1, k1) 11 times	
Round 6	K88	
Round 7	K88	
Round 8	K88	
Round 9	K88	
Round 10	K88	
Round 11	K88	
Round 12	K88	

Round	Stitch Pattern	Done
Letter		
Round 1	K25, *customize* 10, k4, *customize* 10, k4, *customize* 10, k25	
Round 2	K25, *customize* 10, k4, *customize* 10, k4, *customize* 10, k25	
Round 3	K25, *customize* 10, k4, *customize* 10, k4, *customize* 10, k25	
Round 4	K25, *customize* 10, k4, *customize* 10, k4, *customize* 10, k25	
Round 5	K25, *customize* 10, k4, *customize* 10, k4, *customize* 10, k25	
Round 6	K25, *customize* 10, k4, *customize* 10, k4, *customize* 10, k25	

Round	Stitch Pattern	
Round 7	K25, *customize* 10, k4, *customize* 10, k4, *customize* 10, k25	
Round 8	K25, *customize* 10, k4, *customize* 10, k4, *customize* 10, k25	
Round 9	K25, *customize* 10, k4, *customize* 10, k4, *customize* 10, k25	
Round 10	K25, *customize* 10, k4, *customize* 10, k4, *customize* 10, k25	
Round 11	K25, *customize* 10, k4, *customize* 10, k4, *customize* 10, k25	
Round 12	K25, *customize* 10, k4, *customize* 10, k4, *customize* 10, k25	
Round 13	K25, *customize* 10, k4, *customize* 10, k4, *customize* 10, k25	
Round 14	K25, *customize* 10, k4, *customize* 10, k4, *customize* 10, k25	

Top Border

Round	Stitch Pattern
Round 1	K88
Round 2	K88
Round 3	K88
Round 4	K88
Round 5	K88
Round 6	K88
Round 7	(K4, p1, k1, p1, k1) 11 times
Round 8	(K4, k1, p1, k1, p1) 11 times
Round 9	(K4, p1, k1, p1, k1) 11 times
Round 10	(K4, k1, p1, k1, p1) 11 times
Round 11	(K4, p1, k1, p1, k1) 11 times
Round 12	(K4, k1, p1, k1, p1) 11 times

Cast off 88 stitches and secure loose threads.

Notes

Baby Patterns

GIRL CAP

Circular Needle

Yarn: Mary Jo Cole, 100% cashmere

Yards Required: 65

Needles: US 8 (5mm), 16 inch circular, 1 US 8 (5mm) single-point, 4 US 8 (5mm) double-points

Gauge: 12 stitches and 16 rows equal 2.5 inches

Finished Size: 6.5 inches tall and 8.5 inches diameter

Abbreviations: K (k): Knit; P (p): Purl;
SSK (ssk): Slide two stitches, one at a time, from left needle to right as if you were going to knit them. Insert the left needle through the two stitches and knit them together through the back.

Cast on 64 stitches of trim color on a straight needle and then transfer them to the circular one. Place a marker in front of first stitch to indicate beginning of the row. Join for knitting in the round.

jil eaton Minnow Merino, 100% extra fine merino wool with a gauge of 4.5 stitches to one inch is a wonderful alternative yarn for this project.

Round	Stitch Pattern	Total # of Stitches	Done
Round 1	K64	64	✓
Round 2	K64	64	
Round 3	K64	64	
Round 4	K64	64	
Round 5	K64	64	
Round 6	K64	64	
Round 7	K64	64	
Round 8	K64	64	

Change yarn to main color.

Round	Stitch Pattern	Total # of Stitches	Done
Round 9	K64	64	

Round	Stitch Pattern	Total # of Stitches	Done
"L" · · · "R" · · · "I" · · · "G"			
Round 1	K9, p10, k2, p3, k4, p3, k2, p10, k2, k1, p8, k1, k9	64	
Round 2	K9, p10, k2, p3, k4, p3, k2, p10, k2, p10, k9	64	
Round 3	K9, p10, k2, k1, p3, k3, p3, k2, p10, k2, p3, k4, p3, k9	64	

Round	Stitch Pattern	Total # of Stitches	Done
Round 4	K9, k7, p3, k2, k1, p3, k3, p3, k2, k3, p4, k3, k2, k1, p3, k3, p3, k9	64	
Round 5	K9, k7, p3, k2, k2, p3, k2, p3, k2, k3, p4, k3, k2, k1, p3, k3, p3, k9	64	
Round 6	K9, k7, p3, k2, k2, p3, k2, p3, k2, k3, p4, k3, k2, p5, k2, p3, k9	64	
Round 7	K9, k7, p3, k2, k3, p7, k2, k3, p4, k3, k2, p5, k2, p3, k9	64	
Round 8	K9, k7, p3, k2, k2, p8, k2, k3, p4, k3, k2, k7, p3, k9	64	
Round 9	K9, k7, p3, k2, k1, p2, k4, p3, k2, k3, p4, k3, k2, k7, p3, k9	64	
Round 10	K9, k7, p3, k2, p3, k4, p3, k2, k3, p4, k3, k2, p3, k4, p3, k9	64	
Round 11	K9, k7, p3, k2, p4, k3, p3, k2, k3, p4, k3, k2, p3, k4, p3, k9	64	
Round 12	K9, k7, p3, k2, p10, k2, p10, k2, p10, k9	64	
Round 13	K9, k7, p3, k2, k1, p9, k2, p10, k2, p10, k9	64	
Round 14	K9, k7, p3, k2, k2, p8, k2, p10, k2, k1, p8, k1, k9	64	

Start Crown

Round	Stitch Pattern	Total # of Stitches	Done
Round 1	K64	64	
Round 2	(K6, ssk) 8 times	56	
Round 3	K56	56	
Round 4	(K5, ssk) 8times	48	
Round 5	K48	48	
Round 6	(K4, ssk) 8 times	40	
Round 7	K40	40	

Transfer stitches to three double-point needles and use the fourth to knit with.

Round	Stitch Pattern	Total # of Stitches	Done
Round 8	(K3, ssk) 8 times	32	
Round 9	K32	32	
Round 10	(K2, ssk) 8 times	24	
Round 11	K24	24	
Round 12	(K1, ssk) 8 times	16	
Round 13	K16	16	
Round 14	SSK 8 times	8	
Round 15	K8	8	
Round 16	SSK 4 times	4	

Change to trim color and knit I-cord on the remaining stitches as follows:

K4, slide the stitches to the other end of the needle, bring the yarn from behind and knit the stitches again. Repeat for desired length.

I-cord length is a matter of preference, but approximately 4 inches works well. I like it long and floppy as opposed to short and tight. Bind off 4 stitches and secure loose threads on the inside.

Image on page 119.

BOY CAP

Circular
Needle

Yarn: Mary Jo Cole, 100% cashmere

Yards Required: 65

Needles: US 8 (5mm), 16 inch circular, 1 US 8 (5mm) single-point, 4 US 8 (5mm) double-points

Gauge: 12 stitches and 16 rows equal 2.5 inches

Finished Size: 6.5 inches tall and 8.5 inches diameter

Abbreviations: K (k): Knit; P (p): Purl;
SSK (ssk): Slide two stitches, one at a time, from left needle to right as if you were going to knit them. Insert the left needle through the two stitches and knit them together through the back.

Cast on 64 stitches of trim color on a straight needle and then transfer them to the circular one. Place a marker in front of first stitch to indicate beginning of the row. Join for knitting in the round.

jil eaton Minnow Merino, 100% extra fine merino wool with a gauge of 4.5 stitches to one inch is a wonderful alternative yarn for this project.

Round	Stitch Pattern	Total # of Stitches	Done
Round 1	K64	64	✓
Round 2	K64	64	
Round 3	K64	64	
Round 4	K64	64	
Round 5	K64	64	
Round 6	K64	64	
Round 7	K64	64	
Round 8	K64	64	

Change yarn to main color.

Round	Stitch Pattern	Total # of Stitches	Done
Round 9	K64	64	

Round	Stitch Pattern	Total # of Stitches	Done
"Y" ... "O" ... "B"			
Round 1	K10, k4, p2, k4, k7, k3, p4, k3, k7, k2, p8, k10	64	
Round 2	K10, k4, p2, k4, k7, k2, p6, k2, k7, k1, p9, k10	64	
Round 3	K10, k4, p2, k4, k7, k1, p8, k1, k7, p10, k10	64	
Round 4	K10, k4, p2, k4, k7, p3, k4, p3, k7, p4, k3, p3, k10	64	
Round 5	K10, k4, p2, k4, k7, p3, k4, p3, k7, p3, k4, p3, k10	64	

Round	Stitch Pattern	Total # of Stitches	Done
Round 6	K10, k3, p4, k3, k7, p3, k4, p3, k7, k1, p2, k4, p3, k10	64	
Round 7	K10, k3, p4, k3, k7, p3, k4, p3, k7, k2, p8, k10	64	
Round 8	K10, k2, p6, k2, k7, p3, k4, p3, k7, k2, p8, k10	64	
Round 9	K10, k2, p2, k2, p2, k2, k7, p3, k4, p3, k7, k1, p2, k4, p3, k10	64	
Round 10	K10, k2, p2, k2, p2, k2, k7, p3, k4, p3, k7, p3, k4, p3, k10	64	
Round 11	K10, k1, p3, k2, p3, k1, k7, p3, k4, p3, k7, p4, k3, p3, k10	64	
Round 12	K10, k1, p3, k2, p3, k1, k7, k1, p8, k1, k7, p10, k10	64	
Round 13	K10, p3, k4, p3, k7, k2, p6, k2, k7, k1, p9, k10	64	
Round 14	K10, p3, k4, p3, k7, k3, p4, k3, k7, k2, p8, k10	64	

Start Crown

Round	Stitch Pattern	Total # of Stitches	Done
Round 1	K64	64	
Round 2	(K6, ssk) 8 times	56	
Round 3	K56	56	
Round 4	(K5, ssk) 8 times	48	
Round 5	K48	48	
Round 6	(K4, ssk) 8 times	40	
Round 7	K40	40	

Transfer stitches to three double-point needles and knit with the fourth.

Round	Stitch Pattern	Total # of Stitches	Done
Round 8	(K3, ssk) 8 times	32	
Round 9	K32	32	
Round 10	(K2, ssk) 8 times	24	
Round 11	K24	24	
Round 12	(K1, ssk) 8 times	16	
Round 13	K16	16	
Round 14	SSK 8 times	8	
Round 15	K8	8	
Round 16	SSK 4 times	4	

Change to trim color and knit I-cord on the 4 remaining stitches as follows:

K4, slide the stitches to the other end of the needle, bring the yarn from behind and knit the stitches again. Repeat for desired length.

I-cord length is a matter of preference, but approximately 4 inches works well. I like it long and floppy as opposed to short and tight. Bind off 4 stitches and secure loose threads on the inside.

Image on page 119.

When customizing your own 3-letter name or initial, work the stitches from right to left and bottom to top.

CONTRAST G CAP

Single-Point Needles

Yarn: Mary Jo Cole, 100% cashmere

Yards Required: 65

Needles: US 8 (5mm) single-point,
4 US 8 (5mm) double-points (for I-cord)

Gauge: 12 stitches and 16 rows equal 2.5 inches

Finished Size: 6.5 inches tall and 8.5 inches diameter

Abbreviations: K (k): Knit; P (p): Purl;
SSK (ssk): Slide two stitches, one at a time, from left needle to right as
if you were going to knit them. Insert the left needle through the two
stitches and knit them together through the back;
MC: Main Color; TC: Trim Color

Cast on 64 stitches of trim color on a straight needle.

jil eaton Minnow Merino, 100% extra fine merino wool with a gauge of 4.5 stitches to one inch is a wonderful alternative yarn for this project.

Row	Stitch Pattern	Total # of Stitches	Done
Row 1	K64 TC	64	✓
Row 2	P64 TC	64	
Row 3	K64 TC	64	
Row 4	P64 TC	64	
Row 5	K64 TC	64	
Row 6	P64 TC	64	
Row 7	K64 TC	64	
Row 8	P64 TC	64	

Change yarn to Main Color.

Row	Stitch Pattern	Total # of Stitches	Done
Row 9	K64 MC	64	

Row	Stitch Pattern	Total # of Stitches	Done
"G"			
Row 1	P27 MC, p1 MC, p8 TC, p1 MC, p27 MC	64	
Row 2	K27 MC, k10 TC, k27 MC	64	
Row 3	P27 MC, p3 TC, p4 MC, p3 TC, p27 MC	64	
Row 4	K27 MC, k1 MC, k3 TC, k3 MC, k3 TC, k27 MC	64	

Row	Stitch Pattern	Total # of Stitches	Done
Row 5	P27 MC, p3 TC, p3 MC, p3 TC, p1 MC, p27 MC	64	
Row 6	K27 MC, k5 TC, k2 MC, k3 TC, k 27 MC	64	
Row 7	P27 MC, p3 TC, p2 MC, p5 TC, p27 MC	64	
Row 8	K27 MC, k7 MC, k3 TC, k27 MC	64	
Row 9	P27 MC, p3 TC, p7 MC, p27 MC	64	
Row 10	K27 MC, k3 TC, k4 MC, k3 TC, k27 MC	64	
Row 11	P27 MC, p3 TC, p4 MC, p3 TC, p27 MC	64	
Row 12	K27 MC, k10 TC, k27 MC	64	
Row 13	P27 MC, p10 TC, p27 MC	64	
Row 14	K27 MC, k1 MC, k8 TC, k1 MC, k27 MC	64	

When the first row of the letter is complete, tie the ends of the main and trim colors together on the wrong side, then weave them in when the cap is completed.

Start Crown

Row	Stitch Pattern	Total # of Stitches	Done
Row 1	P64 MC	64	
Row 2	(K6, ssk) MC 8 times	56	
Row 3	P56 MC	56	
Row 4	(K5, ssk) MC 8 times	48	
Row 5	P48 MC	48	
Row 6	(K4, ssk) MC 8 times	40	
Row 7	P40 MC	40	
Row 8	(K3, ssk) MC 8 times	32	
Row 9	P32 MC	32	
Row 10	(K2, ssk) MC 8 times	24	
Row 11	P24 MC	24	
Row 12	(K1, ssk) MC 8 times	16	
Row 13	P16 MC	16	
Row 14	SSK MC 8 times	8	
Row 15	P8 MC	8	
Row 16	SSK MC 4 times	4	

Change to trim color and knit I-cord on the 4 remaining stitches as follows:

K4, slide the stitches to the other end of the needle, bring the yarn from behind and knit the stitches again. Repeat for desired length.

I-cord length is a matter of preference, but approximately 4 inches works well. I like it long and floppy as opposed to short and tight. Bind off 4 stitches and secure loose threads on the inside. Sew up back of hat.

Image on page 125.

CONTRAST B CAP

Single-Point Needles

Yarn: Mary Jo Cole, 100% cashmere

Yards Required: 65

Needles: US 8 (5mm) single-point,
4 US 8 (5mm) double-points (for I-cord)

Gauge: 12 stitches and 16 rows equal 2.5 inches

Finished Size: 6.5 inches tall and 8.5 inches diameter

Abbreviations: K (k): Knit; P (p): Purl;
SSK (ssk): Slide two stitches, one at a time, from left needle to right as if you were going to knit them. Insert the left needle through the two stitches and knit them together through the back;
MC: Main Color; TC: Trim Color

Cast on 64 stitches of trim color on a straight needle.

jil eaton Minnow Merino, 100% extra fine merino wool with a gauge of 4.5 stitches to one inch is a wonderful alternative yarn for this project.

Row	Stitch Pattern	Total # of Stitches	Done
Row 1	K64 TC	64	✓
Row 2	P64 TC	64	
Row 3	K64 TC	64	
Row 4	P64 TC	64	
Row 5	K64 TC	64	
Row 6	P64 TC	64	
Row 7	K64 TC	64	
Row 8	P64 TC	64	

Change yarn to Main Color.

Row	Stitch Pattern	Total # of Stitches	Done
Row 9	K64 MC	64	

Row	Stitch Pattern	Total # of Stitches	Done
"B"			
Row 1	P27 MC, p8 TC, p2 MC, p27 MC	64	
Row 2	K27 MC, k1 MC, k9 TC, k27 MC	64	
Row 3	P27 MC, p10 TC, p27 MC	64	
Row 4	K27 MC, k4 TC, k3 MC, k3 TC, k27 MC	64	

Row	Stitch Pattern	Total # of Stitches	Done
Row 5	P27 MC, p3 TC, p4 MC, p3 TC, p27 MC	64	
Row 6	K27 MC, k1 MC, k2 TC, k4 MC, k3 TC, k27 MC	64	
Row 7	P27 MC, p8 TC, p2 MC, p27 MC	64	
Row 8	K27 MC, k2 MC, k8 TC, k27 MC	64	
Row 9	P27 MC, p3 TC, p4 MC, p2 TC, p1 MC, p27 MC	64	
Row 10	K27 MC, k3 TC, k4 MC, k3 TC, k27 MC	64	
Row 11	P27 MC, p3 TC, p3 MC, p4 TC, p27 MC	64	
Row 12	K27 MC, k10 TC, k27 MC	64	
Row 13	P27 MC, p9 TC, p1 MC, p27 MC	64	
Row 14	K27 MC, k2 MC, k8 TC, k27 MC	64	

Follow instructions shown for the G cap in order to keep you work as neat and tidy as possible.

Start Crown

Row	Stitch Pattern	Total # of Stitches	Done
Row 1	P64 MC	64	
Row 2	(K6, ssk) MC 8 times	56	
Row 3	P56 MC	56	
Row 4	(K5, ssk) MC 8 times	48	
Row 5	P48 MC	48	
Row 6	(K4, ssk) MC 8 times	40	
Row 7	P40 MC	40	
Row 8	(K3, ssk) MC 8 times	32	
Row 9	P32 MC	32	
Row 10	(K2, ssk) MC 8 times	24	
Row 11	P24 MC	24	
Row 12	(K1, ssk) MC 8 times	16	
Row 13	P16 MC	16	
Row 14	SSK MC 8 times	8	
Row 15	P8 MC	8	
Row 16	SSK MC 4 times	4	

Change to trim color and knit I-cord on the 4 remaining stitches as follows:

K4, slide the stitches to the other end of the needle, bring the yarn from behind and knit the stitches again. Repeat for desired length.

I-cord length is a matter of preference, but approximately 4 inches works well. I like it long and floppy as opposed to short and tight. Bind off 4 stitches and secure loose threads on the inside. Sew up back of hat.

Image on page 124.

BABY CUBE

Single-Point
Needles

Yarn: jil eaton Minnow Merino,
100% extra fine superwash merino wool, 77 yd per 50g

Yards Required: 200

Needles: US 8 (5mm)

Gauge: 18 stitches equals 4 inches

Finished Size: 5.5 inches cubed

Abbreviations: K (k): Knit; P (p): Purl

Row	Stitch Pattern	Done

"B" Square (make 2)

Cast on 22 stitches on a single-point needle.

Below the Letter

Row	Stitch Pattern	Done
Row 1	K22	✓
Row 2	P22	
Row 3	K22	
Row 4	P22	
Row 5	K22	
Row 6	P22	

Row	Stitch Pattern	Done

The Letter

Row	Stitch Pattern	Done
Row 1	K6, k2, p8, k6	
Row 2	P6, k9, p1, p6	
Row 3	K6, p10, k6	
Row 4	P6, k3, p3, k4, p6	
Row 5	K6, p3, k4, p3, k6	
Row 6	P6, k3, p4, k2, p1, p6	
Row 7	K6, k2, p8, k6	
Row 8	P6, k8, p2, p6	
Row 9	K6, k1, p2, k4, p3, k6	
Row 10	P6, k3, p4, k3, p6	
Row 11	K6, k4, k3, p4, k6	
Row 12	P6, k10, p6	
Row 13	K6, k1, p9, k6	
Row 14	P6, k8, p2, p6	

Above the Letter

Row	Stitch Pattern	Done
Row 1	K22	
Row 2	P22	
Row 3	K22	
Row 4	P22	
Row 5	K22	
Row 6	P22	

Cast off 22 stitches and secure loose threads on back.

"A" Square (make one)

Cast on 22 stitches on a single-point needle.

Below the Letter

Row	Stitch Pattern	Done
Row 1	K22	
Row 2	P22	
Row 3	K22	
Row 4	P22	
Row 5	K22	
Row 6	P22	

The Letter

Row	Stitch Pattern	Done
Row 1	K6, p3, k4, p3, k6	
Row 2	P6, k3, p4, k3, p6	
Row 3	K6, p4, k2, p4, k6	
Row 4	P6, k4, p2, k4, p6	
Row 5	K6, k1, p8, k1, k6	
Row 6	P6, p1, k8, p1, p6	
Row 7	K6, p2, k6, p2, k6	
Row 8	P6, p2, k2, p2, k2, p2, p6	
Row 9	K6, k2, p2, k2, p2, k2, k6	
Row 10	P6, p2, k2, p2, k2, p2, p6	

Row	Stitch Pattern	Done
Row 11	K6, k3, p4, k3, k6	
Row 12	P6, p3, k4, p3, k6	
Row 13	K6, k4, p2, k4, k6	
Row 14	P6, p4, k2, p4, p6	

Above the Letter

Row	Stitch Pattern	Done
Row 1	K22	
Row 2	P22	
Row 3	K22	
Row 4	P22	
Row 5	K22	
Row 6	P22	

Cast off 22 stitches and secure loose threads on back.

"Y" Square (make one)

Cast on 22 stitches on a single-point needle.

Below the Letter

Row	Stitch Pattern	Done
Row 1	K22	
Row 2	P22	
Row 3	K22	
Row 4	P22	
Row 5	K22	
Row 6	P22	

The Letter

Row	Stitch Pattern	Done
Row 1	K6, k4, p2, k4, k6	
Row 2	P6, p4, k2, p4, p6	
Row 3	K6, k4, p2, k4, k6	
Row 4	P6, p4, k2, p4, p6	

Row	Stitch Pattern	Done
Row 5	K6, k4, p2, k4, k6	
Row 6	P6, p3, k4, p3, p6	
Row 7	K6 ,k3 ,p4, k3, k6	
Row 8	P6, p2, k6, p2, p6	
Row 9	K6, k2, p2, k2, p2, k2, k6	
Row 10	P6, p2, k2, p2, k2, p2, p6	
Row 11	K6, k1, p3, k2, p3, k1, k6	
Row 12	P6, p1, k3, p2, k3, p1, p6	
Row 13	K6, p3, k4, p3, k6	
Row 14	P6, k3, p4, k3, k7	

Above the Letter

Row	Stitch Pattern	Done
Row 1	K22	
Row 2	P22	
Row 3	K22	
Row 4	P22	
Row 5	K22	
Row 6	P22	

Cast off 22 stitches and secure loose threads on back.

❤ Square (make 2)

Cast on 22 stitches on a single-point needle.

Below the ❤

Row	Stitch Pattern	Done
Row 1	K22	
Row 2	P22	
Row 3	K22	
Row 4	P22	
Row 5	K22	
Row 6	P22	

The ❤

Row	Stitch Pattern	Done
Row 1	K5, k5, p2, k5, k5	
Row 2	P5, p4, k4, p4, p5	
Row 3	K5, k3, p6, k3, k5	
Row 4	P5, p3, k6, p3, p5	
Row 5	K5, k2, p8, k2, k5	
Row 6	P5, p2, k8, p2, p5	
Row 7	K5, k1, p10, k1, k5	
Row 8	P5, p1, k10, p1, p5	
Row 9	K5, p12, k5	
Row 10	P5, k12, p5	
Row 11	K5, p12, k5	
Row 12	P5, k5, p2, k5, p5	
Row 13	K5, p4, k4, p4, k5	
Row 14	P5, p1, k2, p6, k2, p1, p5	

Above the ❤

Row	Stitch Pattern	Done
Row 1	K22	
Row 2	P22	
Row 3	K22	
Row 4	P22	
Row 5	K22	
Row 6	P22	

Cast off 22 stitches and secure loose threads on back.

Stitch 6 squares beginning with B - A - B - Y side by side and then attaching a Heart on the top. Fill the five-sided cube with foam, down or your choice of stuffing, and then attach the other heart, the sixth side, on the bottom.

This is the perfect shape for a six-letter name or a four-letter name with the heart on the top and the bottom. Knit a Baby cube and a Love cube for the perfect shower gift.

LOVE CUBE

Single-Point
Needles

Yarn: jil eaton Minnow Merino,
100% extra fine superwash merino wool,
77 yd per 50g

Yards Required: 200

Needles: US 8 (5mm)

Gauge: 18 stitches equals 4 inches

Finished Size: 5.5 inches cubed

Abbreviations: K (k): Knit; P (p): Purl

Row	*Stitch Pattern*	*Done*

"L" Square

Cast on 22 stitches on a single-point needle.

Below the Letter

Row	Stitch Pattern	Done
Row 1	K22	✓
Row 2	P22	
Row 3	K22	
Row 4	P22	
Row 5	K22	
Row 6	P22	

Row	*Stitch Pattern*	*Done*

The Letter

Row	Stitch Pattern	Done
Row 1	K6, p10, k6	
Row 2	P6, k10, p6	
Row 3	K6, p10, k6	
Row 4	P6, k10, p6	
Row 5	K6, p3, k7, k6	
Row 6	P6, p7, k3, p6	
Row 7	K6, p3, k7, k6	
Row 8	P6, p7, k3, p6	
Row 9	K6, p3, k7, k6	
Row 10	P6, p7, k3, p6	
Row 11	K6, p3, k7, k6	
Row 12	P6, p7, k3, p6	
Row 13	K6, p3, k7, k6	
Row 14	P6, p7, k3, p6	

Above the Letter

Row	Stitch Pattern	Done
Row 1	K22	
Row 2	P22	
Row 3	K22	
Row 4	P22	
Row 5	K22	
Row 6	P22	

Cast off 22 stitches and secure loose threads on back.

"O" Square

Cast on 22 stitches on a single-point needle.

Below the Letter

Row	Stitch Pattern	Done
Row 1	K22	
Row 2	P22	
Row 3	K22	
Row 4	P22	
Row 5	K22	
Row 6	P22	

The Letter

Row	Stitch Pattern	Done
Row 1	K6, k2, p6, k2, k6	
Row 2	P6, p1, k8, p1, p6	
Row 3	K6, p10, k6	
Row 4	P6, k10, p6	
Row 5	K6, p3, k4, p3, k6	
Row 6	P6, k3, p4, k3, p6	
Row 7	K6, p3, k4, p3, k6	
Row 8	P6, k3, p4, k3, p6	
Row 9	K6, p3, k4, p3, k6	

Row	Stitch Pattern	Done
Row 10	P6, k3, p4, k3, p6	
Row 11	K6, p10, k6	
Row 12	P6, k10, p6	
Row 13	K6, k1, p8, k1, k6	
Row 14	P6, p2, k6, p2, p6	

Above the Letter

Row	Stitch Pattern	Done
Row 1	K22	
Row 2	P22	
Row 3	K22	
Row 4	P22	
Row 5	K22	
Row 6	P22	

"V" Square

Cast on 22 stitches on a single-point needle.

Below the Letter

Row	Stitch Pattern	Done
Row 1	K22	
Row 2	P22	
Row 3	K22	
Row 4	P22	
Row 5	K22	
Row 6	P22	

The Letter

Row	Stitch Pattern	Done
Row 1	P6, k4, p2, k4, p6	
Row 2	K6, p4, k2, p4, k6	
Row 3	P6, k3, p4, k3, p6	
Row 4	K6, p3, k4, p3, k6	
Row 5	P6, k2, p2, k2, p2, k2, p6	
Row 6	K6, p2, k2, p2, k2, p2, k6	

Row 7	P6, k2, p2, k2, p2, k2, p6
Row 8	K6, p1, k2, p4, k2, p1, k6
Row 9	P6, k1, p2, k4, p2, k1, p6
Row 10	K6, p1, k2, p4, k2, p1, k6
Row 11	P6, p2, k6, p2, p6
Row 12	K6, k2, p6, k2, k6
Row 13	P6, p2, k6, p2, p6
Row 14	K6, k2, p6, k2, k6

Above the Letter

Row 1	K22
Row 2	P22
Row 3	K22
Row 4	P22
Row 5	K22
Row 6	P22

Cast off 22 stitches and secure loose threads on back.

"E" Square

Cast on 22 stitches on a single-point needle.

Below the Letter

Row 1	K22
Row 2	P22
Row 3	K22
Row 4	P22
Row 5	K22
Row 6	P22

The Letter

Row 1	K6, p10, k6
Row 2	P6, k10, p6
Row 3	K6, p10, k6
Row 4	P6, p7, k3, p6
Row 5	K6, p3, k7, k6
Row 6	P6, p4, k6, p6
Row 7	K6, p6, k4, k6
Row 8	P6, p3, k7, p6
Row 9	K6, p6, k4, k6
Row 10	P6, p7, k3, p6
Row 11	K6, p3, k7, k6
Row 12	P6, k10, p6
Row 13	K6, p10, k6
Row 14	P6, k10, p6

Above the Letter

Row 1	K22
Row 2	P22
Row 3	K22
Row 4	P22
Row 5	K22
Row 6	P22

Cast off 22 stitches and secure loose threads on back.

♥ Square (make 2)

Cast on 22 stitches on a single-point needle.

Below the 🖤

Row	Stitch Pattern	Done
Row 1	K22	
Row 2	P22	
Row 3	K22	
Row 4	P22	
Row 5	K22	
Row 6	P22	

The 🖤

Row	Stitch Pattern	Done
Row 1	K5, k5, p2, k5, k5	
Row 2	P5, p4, k4, p4, p5	
Row 3	K5, k3, p6, k3, k5	
Row 4	P5, p3, k6, p3, p5	
Row 5	K5, k2, p8, k2, k5	
Row 6	P5, p2, k8, p2, p5	
Row 7	K5, k1, p10, k1, k5	
Row 8	P5, p1, k10, p1, p5	
Row 9	K5, p12, k5	
Row 10	P5, k12, p5	
Row 11	K5, p12, k5	
Row 12	P5, k5, p2, k5, p5	
Row 13	K5, p4, k4, p4, k5	
Row 14	P5, p1, k2, p6, k2, p1, p5	

Above the 🖤

Row	Stitch Pattern	Done
Row 1	K22	
Row 2	P22	
Row 3	K22	
Row 4	P22	
Row 5	K22	
Row 6	P22	

Cast off 22 stitches and secure loose threads on back.

Stitch 6 squares beginning with L - O - V - E side by side and then attaching a heart on the top. Fill the five-sided cube with foam, down or your choice of stuffing, and then attach the other heart, the sixth side, on the bottom.

This is the perfect shape for a six-letter name or a four-letter name with the heart on the top and the bottom. Knit a Baby cube and a Love cube for the perfect shower gift.

I ♥ U CAP

Circular
Needle

Yarn: jil eaton Minnow Merino,
100% extra fine superwash merino wool,
77 yd per 50g

Yards Required: 200

Needles: US 8 (5mm), 16 inch circular,
1 US 8 (5mm) single-point, 4 US 8 (5mm) double-points

Gauge: 18 stitches equal 4 inches

Finished Size: 6.5 inches tall and 8.5 inches diameter

Abbreviations: K (k): Knit; P (p): Purl;
SSK (ssk): Slide two stitches, one at a time, from left needle to right as
if you were going to knit them. Insert the left needle through the two
stitches and knit them together through the back.

Cast on 64 stitches on a straight needle and then transfer them to the
circular one. Place a marker in front of first stitch to indicate beginning
of the row. Join for knitting in the round.

Round	Stitch Pattern	Total # of Stitches	Done
Round 1	K64	64	✓
Round 2	K64	64	
Round 3	K64	64	
Round 4	K64	64	
Round 5	K64	64	
Round 6	K64	64	
Round 7	K64	64	
Round 8	K64	64	
Round 9	K64	64	

Round	Stitch Pattern	Total # of Stitches	Done
"U" . . . "♥" . . . "I"			
Round 1	K8, k2, p6, k2, k8, k5, p2, k5, k8, p10, k8	64	
Round 2	K8, k1, p8, k1, k8, k4, p4, k4, k8, p10, k8	64	
Round 3	K8, p10, k8, k3, p6, k3, k8, p10, k8	64	
Round 4	K8, p3, k4, p3, k8, k3, p6, k3, k8, k3, p4, k3, k8	64	

Round	Stitch Pattern	Total # of Stitches	Done
Round 5	K8, p3, k4, p3, k8, k2, p8, k2, k8, k3, p4, k3, k8	64	
Round 6	K8, p3, k4, p3, k8, k2, p8, k2, k8, k3, p4, k3, k8	64	
Round 7	K8, p3, k4, p3, k8, k1, p10, k1, k8, k3, p4, k3, k8	64	
Round 8	K8, p3, k4, p3, k8, k1, p10, k1, k8, k3, p4, k3, k8	64	
Round 9	K8, p3, k4, p3, k8, p12, k8, k3, p4, k3, k8	64	
Round 10	K8, p3, k4, p3, k8, p12, k8, k3, p4, k3, k8	64	
Round 11	K8, p3, k4, p3, k8, p12, k8, k3, p4, k3, k8	64	
Round 12	K8, p3, k4, p3, k8, p5, k2, p5, k8, p10, k8	64	
Round 13	K8, p3, k4, p3, k8, p4, k4, p4, k8, p10, k8	64	
Round 14	K8, p3, k4, p3, k8, k1, p2, k6, p2, k1, k8, p10, k8	64	

Start Crown

Round	Stitch Pattern	Total # of Stitches	Done
Round 1	K64	64	
Round 2	(K6, ssk) 8 times	56	
Round 3	K56	56	

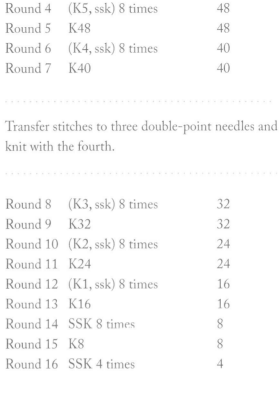

Please note that the middle "letter" is a heart motif so instead of the usual 10-stitch letter layout, it is 12 stitches.

Round	Stitch Pattern	Total # of Stitches	Done
Round 4	(K5, ssk) 8 times	48	
Round 5	K48	48	
Round 6	(K4, ssk) 8 times	40	
Round 7	K40	40	

Transfer stitches to three double-point needles and knit with the fourth.

Round	Stitch Pattern	Total # of Stitches	Done
Round 8	(K3, ssk) 8 times	32	
Round 9	K32	32	
Round 10	(K2, ssk) 8 times	24	
Round 11	K24	24	
Round 12	(K1, ssk) 8 times	16	
Round 13	K16	16	
Round 14	SSK 8 times	8	
Round 15	K8	8	
Round 16	SSK 4 times	4	

Knit I-cord on the 4 remaining stitches as follows:

K4, slide the stitches to the other end of the needle, bring the yarn from behind and knit the stitches again. Repeat for desired length. I-cord length is a matter of preference, but approximately 4 inches works well. I like it long and floppy as opposed to short and tight. Bind off 4 stitches and secure loose threads on the inside.

I ♥ U SCARF

Yarn: jil eaton Minnow Merino,
100% extra fine superwash merino wool,
77 yd per 50g

Yards Required: 100

Needles: US 8 (5mm)

Gauge: 18 stitches equal 4 inches

Finished Size: 22 inches long and 5 inches wide

Abbreviations: K (k): Knit; P (p): Purl

Cast on 22 stitches on a straight needle.

Row	Stitch Pattern	Done
Outside Border		
Row 1	K22	✓
Row 2	K22	
Row 3	K22	
Row 4	K22	
Row 5	K22	
Row 6	K22	
Letter "U"		
(Bottom of wearer's right side)		
Row 1	K6, k2, p6, k2, k6	
Row 2	K6, p1, k8, p1, k6	

Row	Stitch Pattern	Done
Row 3	K6, p10, k6	
Row 4	K6, k3, p4, k3, k6	
Row 5	K6, p3, k4, p3, k6	
Row 6	K6, k3, p4, k3, k6	
Row 7	K6, p3, k4, p3, k6	
Row 8	K6, k3, p4, k3, k6	
Row 9	K6, p3, k4, p3, k6	
Row 10	K6, k3, p4, k3, k6	
Row 11	K6, p3, k4, p3, k6	
Row 12	K6, k3, p4, k3, k6	
Row 13	K6, p3, k4, p3, k6	
Row14	K6, k3, p4, k3, k6	

Inside Border

Row 1   K22
Row 2   K22
Row 3   K22
Row 4   K22

❤ Motif

(The heart has 12 stitches not 10 and is in middle of wearer's right side)

Row 1   K5, k5, p2, k5, k5
Row 2   K5, p4, k4, p4, k5
Row 3   K5, k3, p6, k3, k5
Row 4   K5, p3, k6, p3, k5
Row 5   K5, k2, p8, k2, k5
Row 6   K5, p2, k8, p2, k5
Row 7   K5, k1, p10, k1, k5
Row 8   K5, p1, k10, p1, k5
Row 9   K5, p12, k5
Row 10   K5, k12, k5
Row 11   K5, p12, k5
Row 12   K5, k5, p2, k5, k5
Row 13   K5, p4, k4, p4, k5
Row 14   K5, p1, k2, p6, k2, p1, k5

Inside Border

Row 1   K22
Row 2   K22
Row 3   K22
Row 4   K22

Bottom of "I"

(Top of wearer's right side)

Row 1   K6, p10, k6
Row 2   K6, k10, k6
Row 3   K6, p10, k6
Row 4   K6, p3, k4, p3, k6
Row 5   K6, k3, p4, k3, k6
Row 6   K6, p3, k4, p3, k6
Row 7   K6, k3, p4, k3, k6
Row 8   K6, p3, k4, p3, k6
Row 9   K6, k3, p4, k3, k6
Row 10   K6, p3, k4, p3, k6
Row 11   K6, k3, p4, k3, k6
Row 12   K6, k10, k6
Row 13   K6, p10, k6
Row 14   K6, k10, k6

Back of Neck

Row 1   K22
Row 2   K22
Row 3   K22
Row 4   K22
Row 5   K22
Row 6   K22
Row 7   K22
Row 8   K22
Row 9   K22
Row 10   K22
Row 11   K22
Row 12   K22
Row 13   K22
Row 14   K22
Row 15   K22
Row 16   K22
Row 17   K22
Row 18   K22

Row	Stitch Pattern	Done
Row 19	K22	
Row 20	K22	
Row 21	K22	
Row 22	K22	
Row 23	K22	
Row 24	K22	
Row 25	K22	
Row 26	K22	
Row 27	K22	
Row 28	K22	
Row 29	K22	
Row 30	K22	
Row 31	K22	
Row 32	K22	
Row 33	K22	
Row 34	K22	
Row 35	K22	
Row 36	K22	
Row 37	K22	
Row 38	K22	
Row 39	K22	
Row 40	K22	

Top of "I"

(Top of wearer's left side)

Row	Stitch Pattern	Done
Row 1	K6, p10, k6	
Row 2	K6, k10, k6	
Row 3	K6, p10, k6	
Row 4	K6, p3, k4, p3, k6	
Row 5	K6, k3, p4, k3, k6	
Row 6	K6, p3, k4, p3, k6	
Row 7	K6, k3, p4, k3, k6	
Row 8	K6, p3, k4, p3, k6	
Row 9	K6, k3, p4, k3, k6	
Row 10	K6, p3, k4, p3, k6	
Row 11	K6, k3, p4, k3, k6	
Row 12	K6, k10, k6	

Row	Stitch Pattern	Done
Row 13	K6, p10, k6	
Row 14	K6, k10, k6	

Inside Border

Row	Stitch Pattern	Done
Row 1	K22	
Row 2	K22	
Row 3	K22	
Row 4	K22	

❤ Motif

(The heart has 12 stitches not 10 and will appear in middle of wearer's left side)

Row	Stitch Pattern	Done
Row 1	K5, p1, k2, p6, k2, p1, k5	
Row 2	K5, p4, k4, p4, k5	
Row 3	K5, k5, p2, k5, k5	
Row 4	K5, p12, k5	
Row 5	K5, k12, k5	
Row 6	K5, p12, k5	
Row 7	K5, p1, k10, p1, k5	
Row 8	K5, k1, p10, k1, k5	
Row 9	K5, p2, k8, p2, k5	
Row 10	K5, k2, p8, k2, k5	
Row 11	K5, p3, k6, p3, k5	
Row 12	K5, k3, p6 ,k3, k5	
Row 13	K5, p4, k4, p4, k5	
Row 14	K5, k5, p2, k5, k5	

Inside Border

Row	Stitch Pattern	Done
Row 1	K22	
Row 2	K22	
Row 3	K22	
Row 4	K22	

Top of "U"

(Bottom of wearer's left side)

Row	Stitch Pattern
Row 1	K6, k3, p4, k3, k6
Row 2	K6, p3, k4, p3, k6
Row 3	K6, k3, p4, k3, k6
Row 4	K6, p3, k4, p3, k6
Row 5	K6, k3, p4, k3, k6
Row 6	K6, p3, k4, p3, k6
Row 7	K6, k3, p4, k3, k6
Row 8	K6, p3, k4, p3, k6
Row 9	K6, k3, p4, k3, k6
Row 10	K6, p3, k4, p3, k6
Row 11	K6, k3, p4, k3, k6
Row 12	K6, p10, k6
Row 13	K6, p1, k8, p1, k6
Row 14	K6, k2, p6, k2, k6

Outside Border

Row	Stitch Pattern
Row 1	K22
Row 2	K22
Row 3	K22
Row 4	K22
Row 5	K22
Row 6	K22

Bind off 22 stitches and secure loose threads.

✳ The knit side of this garment is the "face" as it shows the letters off best with the garter stitch trims and background. The I and the U can easily be changed to customize two initials of your favorite child.

SOLID THUMBLESS BABY MITTEN

Yarn: jil eaton Minnow Merino,
100% extra fine superwash merino wool, 77 yd per 50g

Yards Required: 25

Needles: US 8 (5mm)

Gauge: 18 stitches and 24 rows equal 4 inches

Finished Size: 4 inches long and 2.5 inches wide

Abbreviations: K (k): Knit; P (p): Purl;
inc 1: Knit into the front and back of the next stitch (one stitch increased);
k2tog: Knit 2 stitches together as one (one stitch decreased);
p2tog: Purl 2 stitches together as one (one stitch decreased).

Cast on 16 stitches on a single-point needle.

Row	Stitch Pattern	Total # of Stitches	Done	Row	Stitch Pattern	Total # of Stitches	Done
Ribbing				**Hand**			
Row 1	(K1, p1) 8 times	16	✓	Row 1	K2, inc 1, k10, inc 1, k2	18	
Row 2	(K1, p1) 8 times	16		Row 2	P18	18	
Row 3	(K1, p1) 8 times	16		Row 3	K2, inc 1, k12, inc 1,k2	20	
Row 4	(K1, p1) 8 times	16		Row 4	P20	20	
Row 5	(K1, p1) 8 times	16		Row 5	K2, inc 1, k14, inc 1, k2	22	
Row 6	(K1, p1) 8 times	16		Row 6	P22	22	
				Row 7	K22	22	
				Row 8	P22	22	
				Row 9	K22	22	
				Row 10	P22	22	

Row	Stitch Pattern	Total # of Stitches
Row 11	K22	22
Row 12	P22	22
Row 13	K22	22
Row 14	P22	22
Row 15	K2tog 11 times	11
Row 16	P2tog 5 times, p1	6
Row 17	K2tog 3 times	3

Cut the yarn and thread the tail onto a darning needle. Pass the yarn through the 3 remaining stitches and secure all loose threads. Sew the mitten together with a seam in the center back. Repeat all steps to make another mitten.

When decreasing stitches, be sure to pull your yarn snugly to prevent any holes from forming. This is a great style to get creative with and use up small leftover bits of yarn.

Consider positive/negative versions on the cuff and hand. You can also knit stripes; always knit an even number of rows for each stripe so it is easier to "float" the yarn from one color to another. When changing from one color to another, anchor the new and old yarn with a single knot on the back side.

♥ MITTEN

Single-Point
Needles

Yarn: jil eaton Minnow Merino,
100% extra fine superwash merino wool,
77 yd per 50g

Yards Required: 25

Needles: US 8 (5mm)

Gauge: 18 stitches and 24 rows equal 4 inches

Finished Size: 4 inches long and 2.5 inches wide

Abbreviations: K (k): Knit; P (p): Purl;
inc 1: Knit into the front and back of the next stitch (one stitch increased);
k2tog: Knit 2 stitches together as one (one stitch decreased);
p2tog: Purl 2 stitches together as one (one stitch decreased).

Cast on 16 stitches on a single-point needle.

This heart is a hybrid due to the small size of the mitten. It does not appear in any grid and is 8 stitches horizontally and 10 rows vertically.

Row	Stitch Pattern	Total # of Stitches	Done
Ribbing			
Row 1	(K1, p1) 8 times	16	✓
Row 2	(K1, p1) 8 times	16	
Row 3	(K1, p1) 8 times	16	
Row 4	(K1, p1) 8 times	16	
Row 5	(K1, p1) 8 times	16	
Row 6	(K1, p1) 8 times	16	

Row	Stitch Pattern	Total # of Stitches	Done
Hand			
Row 1	K2, inc 1, k10, inc 1, k2	18	
Row 2	P18	18	
♥			
Row 3	K2, inc 1, k2, k1, p2, k2, p2, k1, k2, inc 1, k2	20	
Row 4	P6, k8, p6	20	
Row 5	K2, inc 1, k3, p8, k3, inc 1, k2	20 22	

Row	Stitch Pattern	Total # of Stitches	Done
Row 6	P7, k8, p7	22	
Row 7	K7, k1, p6, k1, k7	22	
Row 8	P7, p1, k6, p1, p7	22	
Row 9	K7, k1, p6, k1, k7	22	
Row 10	P7, p2, k4, p2, p7	22	
Row 11	K7, k2, p4, k2, k7	22	
Row 12	P7, p3, k2, p3, p7	22	
Row 13	K22	22	
Row 14	P22	22	
Row 15	K2tog 11 times	11	
Row 16	P2tog 5 times, p1	6	
Row 17	K2tog, 3 times	3	

Cut the yarn and thread the tail onto a darning needle. Pass the yarn through the 3 remaining stitches and secure all loose threads. Sew the mitten together with a seam in the center back. Repeat all steps to make another mitten.

Notes

$\mathcal{S}$torage

Knitting is something to enjoy whenever the spirit moves you! Because of this it's important to have your knitting supplies close at hand and not tucked away in a spare room, closet or cupboard.

Sometimes I knit in the kitchen and other times in the den, so it's important to be able to grab quickly what I need. If your supplies are close at hand and you see them easily, you may be inspired when you least expect it.

I have always loved glassware and crystal, so when I became serious about knitting, apothecary jars of all shapes and sizes became the storage vessels for my knitting ingredients.

For many years my collection of yarn spools from old New England knitting machines were on display in my office, with no yarn on them, along with an antique iron I picked up years ago in Jakarta. Now these are wrapped with yarn and clustered in my home for easy access when I sit down to knit.

$\mathscr{L}$eftovers

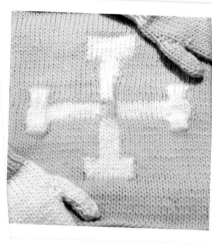

Just like their food counterparts, leftover yarns should be embraced and not thrown out. Many of us have fond memories of suppers where the menu was whatever was left over in the refrigerator. A little of this and a little of that left over often times tastes better than when it was the main course.

Look for a great place to store yarn leftovers and use them to add a bit of unexpected color for a trim, letter or number. I like to use glass apothecary jars to store my leftover yarns; they are attractive and do not need to be hidden away where you will forget about them. Leave them out in the room where you do most of your knitting and you will have constant inspiration to enhance your personalized project.

Decades ago I was a knitwear product manager. One of the sweater companies I worked with designed a sweater each season based on whatever colors were left over from the prior season. The design team was always up to the challenge, and more often than not last season's leftovers turned out to be one of the current season's best sellers.

There's no reason why you cannot embrace a similar philosophy and have your own personalized best seller using leftover yarns in creative combinations.

An adorable striped cap or mittens are great ways to utilize small bits of yarn you may have accumulated. Your imagination is your only limitation.

$\mathscr{S}$hopping

As mentioned in the introduction, yarn type and color are very important to me. My first knitting needles were bamboo and wood, mostly because I thought they were prettier than their metal or plastic counterparts!

I love to shop, as my family, friends and colleagues well know, so finding knitting stores I love to go to, and go back to, is a favorite pastime. This probably has something to do with my career in the fashion business. Imagine being sent to Europe with an expense account to shop for inspiration! That was quite a thrill for a young twenty-something many years ago!

Favorite stores are often local but after a short period of time, and conversation with other knitters, you'll begin to learn of other shops in different parts of the country. It's also great to look for yarn stores prior to vacationing in a new destination. My friend Rosemary, who is from Philadelphia, just told me of a great store called "loop" and I can hardly wait to check it out. Add yarn stores to your address book or PDA devices so that whenever you need to contact your favorite stores, they're ready and available. Here are my local favorites:

Knit & Needlepoint

244 Newbury Street
Boston, MA 02116
(617) 536-9338
www.needlepoint-boston.com

Colorful Stitches

PO Box 2278
48 Main Street
Lenox, MA 01240
(800) 413-6111
colorfulstitches.com

The Creative Stitch

28 South Street
Hingham, MA 02043
(781) 749-2280
www.creativestitchsonline.com

loop

1914 South Street
Philadelphia, PA
(215) 893-9939
www.loopyarn.com

Wool Basket Yarns

19 Depot Street
PO Box 1791
Duxbury, MY 02331
(781) 934-2700
woolbasketyarns.com

SOURCES & OTHER INFORMATION

> Pottery Barn for apothecary jars

> Wisteria for apothecary jars

> Crate and Barrel for apothecary jars

> cspost.com for letter balls

> Michael's for pillow forms and cubes

> *Knitting for Dummies*, 2nd Edition, by Pam Allen, Tracy Barr and Shannon Okey

> YouTube for knitting instructions

> Antique stores for bobbins and knitting spools

> Jakarta stalls for antique iron

> Scalamandre for paw print fabric used for pillow backing

> Schumacher for the blue Asian toile

> Travers for the multi-accessory print

Afterword
A Day in the Life of a Cap

Throughout my career, explaining the functions of the responsibility I held was a fairly regular event. Sometimes, these explanations were written, sometimes they were verbal. Sometimes these explanations were for colleagues, sometimes for government officials. Sometimes these explanations were formal presentations, sometimes they were casual conversations.

At some point I decided to organize into simple steps what I wanted to say. I was in the garment industry speaking to people who wanted to learn more about it, and the industry itself presented an idea that worked well for me over several decades. My document file was known as "A Day in the Life of a Blouse." Every step of the journey a blouse takes from being envisioned by a designer through delivery onto store shelves for the customer to buy was given in varying levels of detail. The focus and greatest detail was on the parts of the process that my team and I were directly accountable for, but it was all-inclusive. I enjoyed formulating the prose and when the idea came to do multiple versions of one project within this workbook, the name and idea were adjusted slightly to have meaning here.

Everyone likes to master something and when you are starting anything new that can be somewhat daunting. In the early stages of my getting more acquainted with knitting and thinking of writing this book, I thought I should pick something I like and master it. I let my imagination run wild; some ideas just did not work, but some ideas are included here. It is my hope that you will enjoy reviewing the variations of the adorable cap and that you master one or more for yourself. Additionally, I hope it provides you with inspiration for creating variations that are a reflection of you and your own creative talent.